American Avalanche Association
and
USDA Forest Service National Avalanche Center

Snow, Weather, and Avalanches: Observation Guidelines for Avalanche Programs in the United States

"Shame shirl"
Bernouli Effect
Zabrooder Film

© American Avalanche Association, 2009

ISBN 0-9760118-1-1

Snow, Weather, and Avalanches:
Observational Guidelines for Avalanche Programs in the United States

Prepared by the Working Group on Observational Guidelines:

Ethan Greene (chair), Colorado Avalanche Information Center
Dale Atkins, Recco AB
Karl Birkeland, USDA Forest Service National Avalanche Center
Kelly Elder, USDA Forest Service Rocky Mountain Research Station
Chris Landry, Center for Snow and Avalanche Studies
Brian Lazar, American Institute for Avalanche Research and Education
Ian McCammon, Snowpit Technologies
Mark Moore, USDA Forest Service Northwest Avalanche Center
Don Sharaf, Valdez Heli-Ski Guides/National Outdoor Leadership School
Craig Sterbenz, Telluride Ski Company
Bruce Tremper, USDA Forest Service Utah Avalanche Center
Knox Williams, Colorado Avalanche Information Center

Issued by:
The American Avalanche Association
P.O. Box 2831
Pagosa Springs, CO 81147
aaa@avalanche.org
www. americanavalancheassociation.org

Front cover photographs by Karl Birkeland, Kelly Elder, Dave Dellamora, Dave Madara, Mark Moore, Mt. Shasta Avalanche Center, Mt. Washington Avalanche Center, Mark Mueller, Ben Pritchett, Billy Rankin, Don Sharaf, John Spitzer, John Stimberis, John Talbott, Bruce Tremper, and .

Back cover photograph by Craig Sterbenz.

Preface

In 2004 the American Avalanche Association, in cooperation with the USDA Forest Service National Avalanche Center, published the inaugural edition of *Snow, Weather and Avalanches: Observational Guidelines for Avalanche Programs in the United States*. Getting to that point was a long and somewhat painful process taking several years, numerous individuals, and many organizations working to find common ground. In the end, the guidelines reflected our community's best effort at merging the Westwide data standards (which had been widely used in the United States since 1968) and the guidelines published by our friends north of the border at the Canadian Avalanche Association. The CAA generously offered their guidelines as a template for ours in the hopes that our two avalanche communities can eventually move toward a common document.

The trepidation we felt with the release of the first edition of these guidelines, which quickly became known as *SWAG,* was unnecessary. It gained immediate acceptance by the U.S. avalanche community, as well as by avalanche workers in many other countries. *SWAG* is now integrated into operations handed out in avalanche classes, and can be found in most patrol rooms and on most forecaster's desks around the country.

SWAG aims to capture the techniques and tools currently being used by U.S. avalanche programs. Since these tools are constantly evolving and being updated, so too must this document. Originally we aimed to update *SWAG* every 5 to 10 years. The fact that we are now producing an updated document only five years after the first edition demonstrates the dynamic nature of our profession. In some sections of this edition you will find mostly minor changes in the form of small corrections, additions, or clarifications. In other sections you'll find more significant changes, such as the addition of increasingly popular block tests that aim to index the fracture propagation propensity of the snowpack. This edition also includes the brand new international snow classification scheme slated to be released this coming winter (Appendix F).

The goal of *SWAG* remains the same. It is meant to be a professional reference that establishes common methods. This benefits everyone by both increasing the ease of communication between operations, and by facilitating the development of long term datasets that will provide future insights into avalanche processes. Despite the changes to the current edition, we aimed to maintain the original tone of *SWAG*. As the late El LaChapelle pointed out nearly thirty years ago, there is no one correct path to an accurate avalanche forecast. Similarly, there is not one set of tools or one set methodology that must be used for avalanche operations. This document recognizes the unique nature of many avalanche programs and their special needs, and strives to provide the flexibility necessary for them to operate effectively while still providing a common language for all of us. Finally, this edition – like the first edition – is not meant to inhibit creativity or innovation. We encourage experimentation and the development of new tests and methods by practitioners and scientists alike, a fact emphasized in the major additions to Chapter 2. Here you will find that some of the new sections came out of M.S. and Ph.D. theses, while others started with discussions in a ski patrol shack.

Ron Perla provided extensive comments on the first edition of SWAG, and when he received his copy he wrote to us that "I believe it's much more than just 'Guidelines for Observations'. It's a valuable reference for a wide variety of avalanche studies. I'll keep it close to my desk together with my very limited collection of references which I expect to consult often." We hope this edition also merits such high praise and that you will find it to be a valuable and useful reference for your avalanche work.

Karl Birkeland
USDA Forest Service National Avalanche Center
Bozeman, Montana
September, 2009

Acknowledgements

This document is a collection of protocols and common practices developed during more than 60 years of avalanche work in the United States. Common practice in the United States, in turn, developed through fruitful collaborations with scientists and practitioners in Canada, Europe, Scandinavia, Asia, and other parts of the world. Although the people that contributed to what is now common practice are too numerous to mention here, their contribution to our field and the methods described within this document is significant.

The first version of this document started with a publication of the Canadian Avalanche Association (CAA) entitled *Observational Guidelines and Recording Standards for Weather, Snowpack, and Avalanches* (OGRS). The CAA has devoted a tremendous amount of time and money towards creating and maintaining that document, which has become a symbol of professional practice in North America. The CAA periodically revises OGRS and we have tried to include some of the changes they instituted during the 2007 revision. I sincerely appreciate the CAA's past and present efforts to promote common practice amongst avalanche programs, and for allowing the U.S. community to benefit from their effort. Within the CAA, Clair Israelson (former CAA, President) and Ian Tomm (CAA, President) both provided us with support and encouragement. Cam Campbell (CAA, Technical Committee) helped us with CAA materials and their experience during the last revision of OGRS. Bruce Jamieson provided both material and insight from the work of the Applied Snow and Avalanche Research group at the University of Calgary.

The American Avalanche Association (AAA) and the USDA Forest Service National Avalanche Center (NAC) provided the majority of the funds and infrastructure to develop this document and complete the first revision. Janet Kellam (AAA, President), Mark Mueller (AAA, Executive Director), and Doug Abromeit (NAC, Director) all contributed to this effort.

A public and technical review process dramatically improved the content of the first version. Although we did not seek assistance from as large a group during the revision, their contribution remains a part of this document. They include: Pat Ahern, Jon Andrews, Dale Atkins, Don Bachman, Hal Boyne, Doug Chabot, Steve Conger, Nolan Doesken, Dave Hamre, Bill Glude, Liam Fitzgerald, Ron Johnson, Chris Joosen, Art Judson, Janet Kellam, Tom Kimbrough, Mark Kozak, Bill Lerch, Chris Lundy, Tom McKee, Art Mears, Peter Martinelli Jr., Rod Newcomb, Ron Perla, and Nancy Pfeiffer. I apologize to anyone that I forgot.

There are some individual contributions that are worthy of mention. Ian McCammon provided the field book figures and snow profile reporting forms. Dale Atkins was very helpful in creating the incident forms in Appendix H and the metadata fields in Appendix C. Dan Judd provided the sample programs in Appendix E. Joyce VanDeWater drew the illustrations in Chapter 2. Charles Fierz allowed us to include the new snow classification (Appendix F) and snow symbol fonts. Many photographers provided images for this publication and they are listed with their contribution.

Lastly I would like to thank the members of the Working Group on Observational Guidelines for their dedication and patience during the development and revision of this document.

Ethan Greene
Working Group on Observational Guidelines, Chairman
September, 2009

Contents

Introduction	1
1.0 Manual Snow and Weather Observations	3
1.1 Introduction	3
1.2 Objectives	3
1.3 Standard Morning Snow and Weather Observation	4
1.4 Manual versus Automated Observations	5
1.5 Time Periods for Manual Snow and Weather Observations	5
1.6 Equipment for Manual Standard Observations	5
1.7 Field Book Notes	6
1.8 Field Weather Observations	6
1.9 Location ✦	6
1.10 Date ✦	6
1.11 Time ✦	6
1.12 Sky Condition ✦	6
1.13 Precipitation Type, Rate, and Intensity ✦	7
1.14 Air Temperature ✦	9
1.14.1 Air Temperature Trend	9
1.15 Relative Humidity	11
1.16 Barometric Pressure at Station	11
1.16.1 Pressure Trend	12
1.17 20 cm Snow Temperature ✦	12
1.18 Surface Penetrability ✦	12
1.19 Form and Size of Surface Snow	13
1.20 Height of Snowpack ✦	14
1.21 Height of New Snow ✦	14
1.21.1 Snow Board Naming Conventions	15
1.22 Water Equivalent of New Snow ✦	16
1.23 Density of New Snow	16
1.24 Rain ✦	17
1.25 Accumulated Precipitation	18
1.26 Wind ✦	18
1.27 Blowing Snow at the Ridge Tops	19
2.0 Snowpack Observations	21
2.1 Introduction	21
2.2 Objectives	21
2.3 Standard Snowpack Observation	22

✦ Sections that describe parameters included in a standard observation.

2.4 Snow Profiles	23
2.4.1 Location	24
2.4.2 Frequency of Observations	26
2.4.3 Equipment	27
2.4.4 Field Procedure	27
2.5 Snowpack Observations	28
2.5.1 Snowpack Temperature	28
2.5.2 Layer Boundaries	28
2.5.3 Snow Hardness	29
2.5.4 Grain Form	30
2.5.5 Grain Size	32
2.5.6 Liquid Water Content	32
2.5.7 Density	33
2.5.8 Strength and Stability Tests	33
2.5.9 Marking the Site	33
2.5.10 Graphical Snow Profile Representation	34
2.6 Characterizing Fractures in Column and Block Tests	36
2.6.1 Shear Quality	37
2.6.2 Fracture Character	38
2.7 Column and Block Tests	37
2.7.1 Site Selection	37
2.7.2 Shovel Shear Test	40
2.7.3 Rutschblock Test	42
2.7.4 Compression Test	45
2.7.5 Deep Tap Test	47
2.7.6 Stuffblock Test	48
2.7.7 Extended Column Test	51
2.7.8 Propagation Saw Test	53
2.8 Slope Cut Testing	55
2.9 Non-Standardized Snow Tests	57
2.9.1 Communicating the Results of Non-Standardized Snow Tests	57
2.9.2 Cantilever Beam Test	57
2.9.3 Loaded Column Test	58
2.9.4 Burp-the-Baby	59
2.9.5 Hand Shear Test	60
2.9.6 Ski Pole Penetrometer	60
2.9.7 Tilt Board Test	61
2.9.8 Shovel Tilt Test	61
2.10 Instrumented Methods	62
2.10.1 Ram Profile	62
2.10.2 Shear Frame	66

3.0 Avalanche Observations	69
3.1 Introduction	69
3.2 Objectives	69
3.3 Identification of Avalanche Paths	69
3.4 Standard Avalanche Observation	70
3.5 Avalanche Path Characteristics	71
3.5.1 Area and Path ✦	71
3.5.2 Aspect ✦	71
3.5.3 Slope Angle ✦	71
3.5.4 Elevation ✦	72
3.6 Avalanche Event Characteristics	72
3.6.1 Date ✦	72
3.6.2 Time ✦	72
3.6.3 Avalanche Type ✦	72
3.6.4 Trigger ✦	73
3.6.5 Size ✦	76
3.6.6 Snow Properties	77
3.6.7 Avalanche Dimensions ✦	78
3.6.8 Location of Avalanche Start ✦	79
3.6.9 Terminus ✦	80
3.6.10 Total Deposit Dimensions	81
3.6.11 Avalanche Runout	81
3.6.12 Coding Avalanche Observations	81
3.6.13 Comments	81
3.7 Multiple Avalanche Events	82
3.8 Additional Observations	83
3.8.1 Avalanche Hazard Mitigation Missions	83
3.8.2 Road and Railway Operations	83
Glossary	85
Appendix A: References	93
Appendix B: Units	96
Appendix C: Metadata	101
Appendix D: Observational Sites for Meteorological Measurements	103
Appendix E: Automated Weather Stations	109
Appendix F: ICSI Classification for Seasonal Snow Cover on the Ground	117
Appendix G: Avalanche Danger, Hazard, and Snow Stability Scales	127
Appendix H: Reporting Avalanche Involvements	133
Appendix I: Symbols and Abbreviations	143
Snow Profile Forms and Conversion Charts	148

✦ *Sections that describe parameters included in a standard observation.*

NOTES: Avy II Fall 2009

Precipitation Factors

Accumulation

Intensity

Type

Maritime: 2"/hr

Intermt- 1"/hr

continental → 3/4"/hr

Precipitation Rates

#. Maritime climate
→ warm fronts are usually
followed by cold fronts

Precipitation intensities

Faceting

Happens between 1°C/cm
Temp range →

Short wave radiation can penetrate ≈ 30 cm into the snow
Recrystallization happens as the snow cools by long wave radiation out of
the snow

snowpilot. ☐→ snopack observations Freeware
. ORG

Orographic Lifting

Adiabatic Lapse Rate
− unsaturated ≈ 10°C per km (5.5°F per 1000 Ft) → Ex Eastern Wa
− saturated ≈ 6°C per km (3.5°F per 1000Ft) → Western Wa

Angle of Repose
angle at which snow wants to slide
changes with snow type → Dry vs wet

Introduction

This document contains a set of guidelines for observing and recording snow, weather, and avalanche phenomena. These guidelines were prepared for programs that contain some type of avalanche forecasting operation, but can be applied to other programs. The guidelines are presented as a resource of common methods and are intended to promote efficient and fruitful communication amongst professional operations and between research and operational communities.

The observations presented in this manual were selected to support active avalanche forecasting programs. Observing these parameters will help avalanche forecasters make informed and predictable decisions, provide current and accurate information, and document methods and reasons for operational decisions. Recording these parameters will assist program managers to document and analyze unusual events, benefit pattern recognition and statistical forecasting methods, and assist research into snow and avalanche phenomena. In addition, there is often little snow and weather data collected in mountainous areas and data collected by avalanche forecasting programs can make important contributions to climatological and mountain systems research. Our hope is that this manual will help forecasters carefully choose the observations that will support their programs, and that those observations will generate high quality and consistent data.

It is unlikely that any one operation will make all of the observations outlined within this document. Individual program managers should select a set of parameters that their staff can observe routinely. Programs with specialized needs may have to look elsewhere for information on additional observations. A set of references is listed in Appendix A for this purpose.

Structure of this Manual

This manual is divided into three chapters and nine appendices. Within each chapter, methods for composing an observational scheme are presented first. A standard observation is presented next, and the remainder of each chapter is devoted to describing detailed methods for observing and recording a particular phenomenon. The appendices provide additional information without distracting from the main topics within the manual.

Units

The avalanche community within the United States typically uses a system of units that combines elements of both the English and International (SI) systems. In this document we have attempted to adhere to the SI system whenever possible. In the United States, personnel of avalanche operations and users of their products may not be familiar with all SI units. For this reason individual programs should choose a unit system that suits their particular application. A recommended system of units, an alternative system of English units, and methods for converting values between the two systems are presented in Appendix B. The most noticeable deviation from the SI system is the unit for elevation. In North America most topographic maps use feet as the unit for elevation. For this reason the recommended unit for elevation remains the foot. Throughout the document the recommended unit appears in the text with the common alternative unit adjacent in parentheses. Long-term data records should be stored in the recommended system of units in Appendix B. Data records submitted to a central database are assumed to be in the recommended system unless otherwise stated in the accompanying metadata file (see Appendix C).

Data Codes and Symbols

Symbols and data codes for many of the observations in this document appear in tables within each section. The use of these codes will save space in field books and on log sheets. Many of the codes in Chapter 1 follow conventions from the meteorological community. The codes in Chapters 2 and 3 were chosen to conform to common methods in the avalanche community and to promote efficient communication.

"Ki-yah" "Kia"

Snow, Weather, and Avalanches

Snow pack – Assessing Hazard

Iniatic → Fracture Iniatic (mechanical instability
  → will addes stress cause failure
    tests → rutschblock, compressi, stuff Block test

Fracture Propogatin (structural instability)
  → will Failure propogate & cause a release?
  → shear test → shovel shear

Analytical Approach → see "integrating .... stability Decisions" Handout

Note:

In the PNW, most fatalities happen during
consideranble avy danger days, Not extreme.
Most people recognize extreme days are too dangerous.
Consideranble days are a combo of good skiing &
considerable danger.

Manual Snow and Weather Observations

1.1 Introduction

Manual observations of snow and weather conditions are an important part of an avalanche forecasting operation. This chapter describes methods for making and recording these observations. Section 1.2 describes observation objectives. Section 1.3 outlines the recommended standard morning snow and weather observation. Sections 1.4 through 1.6 give important background information for planning and implementing observational schemes, Sections 1.7 and 1.8 discuss field observations, and Sections 1.9 through 1.27 describe how to observe and record individual parameters.

1.2 Objectives

Snow and weather observations represent a series of meteorological and snow surface measurements taken at a properly instrumented study plot or in the field (refer to Appendix D - Observation Sites for Meteorological Measurements). Observational data taken at regular intervals provide the basis for recognizing changes in stability of the snow cover and for reporting weather conditions to a meteorological office or regional avalanche center.

Sustained long-term data sets of snow and weather observations can be used to improve avalanche hazard forecasts by statistical and numerical techniques. They also serve to increase climatic knowledge of the area. Observations should be complete, accurate, recorded in a uniform manner, and made routinely. Following an established protocol increases the consistency in the data record, reduces error, and increases the potential for useful interpretation of the data.

Figure 1.1 Alpine weather station in the Colorado Rocky Mountains (photograph by Kelly Elder).

Snow, Weather, and Avalanches

1.3 Standard Morning Snow and Weather Observation

Operations that include an avalanche forecasting program typically observe and record a set of weather and snow parameters daily. These observations should be made at about the same time each day and between 4 am and 10 am local standard time. Many operations will need to observe these parameters more than once per day. A set of suggested fields to observe and record, and a brief explanation are listed below. Detailed information on each of these parameters is available in the sections that follow. Sections that are marked with a ✦ contain information on the parameters listed below. An example record sheet appears in Figure 1.2.

1) *Observation Location*– record the location of the observation site or nearest prominent topographic landmark (mountain, pass, drainage, avalanche path, etc.), political landmark (town, road mile, etc.), or geographic coordinates (latitude/longitude or UTM). If the measurements are made at an established study site, record the site name or number.

2) *Elevation* (ASL)– record the elevation of the observation site in feet (meters) above sea level.

3) *Date* – record the date on which the observation is being made (YYYYMMDD).

4) *Time* – record the local time on the 24-hour clock (0000 – 2359) at which the observation began.

5) *Observer* – record the name or names of the personnel that made the observation.

6) *Sky Conditions*- record the sky conditions as Clear, Few, Scattered, Broken, Overcast, or Obscured (Section 1.12).

7) *Current Weather* – record the precipitation type and rate using the scale and data codes in Section 1.13.

8) *Air Temperature* – record the 24-hour maximum, minimum, and current air temperature to the nearest 0.5 °C (or whole °F) (Section 1.14).

9) *Snow Temperature 20 cm* (or 8 in) – record the snow temperature 20 cm (or 8 in) below the snow surface (Section 1.17).

10) *Surface Penetration* – record the surface penetration to the nearest whole centimeter (or 0.5 inch) as described in Section 1.18.

11) *Total Snow Depth* – record the total depth of snow on the ground to the nearest whole centimeter (or 0.5 inch) (Section 1.20).

12) *24-hour New Snow Depth* – record the depth of the snow that accumulated during the previous 24-hours to the nearest whole centimeter (or 0.5 inch) (Section 1.21).

13) *24-hour New Snow Water Content* – record the water content of the snow that accumulated during the previous 24-hours to the nearest 0.1 mm (or 0.01 inch) (Section 1.22).

14) *24-hour Liquid Precipitation*- record the depth of the liquid precipitation that accumulated during the previous 24 hours to the nearest 0.1 mm (or 0.01 inch) (Section 1.24).

15) *Wind Direction* – observe the wind for at least two minutes and record the average wind direction or use an automated measurement. Record wind direction as N, NE, E, SE, S, SW, W, or NW. If an automated measurement is used, record to the nearest 10 degrees (Section 1.26).

16) *Wind Speed* – observe the wind for at least two minutes and record the average wind speed using the indicators in Section 1.26, or use an automated measurement.

17) *Maximum Wind Gust*- observe the wind for at least two minutes and record the speed of the strongest wind gust, or use an automated measurement. For an automated measurement record the time that the wind gust occurred (Section 1.26).

1.4 Manual versus Automated Observations

Observation networks for avalanche forecasting programs usually involve at least one set of manual observations and one or more automated weather stations. Manual observations can be used to maintain a long-term record and observe and record data not amenable to sensing by automated systems. Automated observations provide unattended continuous weather (and some snowpack) information about a certain region or regions within a forecast or ski area. Automated weather stations can be co-located at study sites where manual weather observations and/or snowpack observations are collected. Programs that maintain a study plot should use data from automated weather stations to augment and not replace manual observations. The following chapter discusses how to make and record manual observations. Details regarding automated snow and weather observations appear in Appendix E.

1.5 Time Periods for Manual Snow and Weather Observations

Observations taken at regular daily times are called *standard observations*. Manual observations are typically carried out in 24-hour, 12-hour, or 6-hour intervals. Data collected at 6-hour intervals beginning at 0000 hours Greenwich Mean Time (also termed Coordinated Universal Time (UTC) or Zulu time (Z)) will conform to climatic data sets. Avalanche forecasting operations typically make two standard observations each day at 0700 and 1600 hours local time, when a 12-hour interval is not possible. The type of operation and availability of observers may necessitate different frequencies and times. In regions that observe Daylight Savings Time, schedules should be adjusted so that the observation time does not change (i.e. use local standard time when recording observations). If observations are made on a 24-hour interval, it is best to make that observation in the morning.

Observations taken between the standard times are referred to as *interval observations*. They are taken when the snow stability is changing rapidly, for example, during a heavy snowfall. Interval observations may contain a few selected observations or a complete set of observations.

Observations taken at irregular times are referred to as *intermittent observations*. They are appropriate for sites that are visited infrequently; visits will typically be more than 24 hours apart and need not be regular (i.e. in a heli-ski operation). Intermittent observations may contain a few selected observations or a complete set of observations. In highway operations, intermittent observations often include *shoot* or *storm* observations to coincide with timing of avalanche control missions or the start and end of particular storm cycles (see Figure 1.2 for sample of field book entry).

It is common for avalanche forecasting operations to collect information for an individual storm event. Observations of snowfall, temperature changes, wind direction and speed, and avalanche activity can be observed for a particular *storm unit*. A storm unit is typically a qualitative increment based on precipitation rates or meteorological events. Operations that choose to use a storm unit may also find it useful to develop a quantitative storm unit definition.

1.6 Equipment for Manual Standard Observations

A snow and weather study plot usually contains the following equipment:

- Stevenson screen for housing thermometers (height adjustable)
- Maximum thermometer
- Minimum thermometer
- One or more snow boards with 1 m (~ 3 ft) rods and base plate with minimum dimensions of 40 cm x 40 cm (~ 15 in) and appropriate labels (Figure 1.4)
- Snow stake, depth marker (graduated in cm (in))
- Ruler (graduated in cm (in))
- Snow sampling tube and weighing scale (graduated in grams or water equivalent), or precipitation gauge
- Large putty knife or plate for cutting snow samples
- Field book and pencil (water resistant paper)

The following additional equipment is useful:
- Hygrothermograph located in a Stevenson screen (Figure 1.3)
- Recording precipitation gauge or rain gauge
- Additional snow boards
- First section of a Ram penetrometer
- Barograph (in the office) or barometer/altimeter
- Anemometer at a separate wind station with radio or cable link to a recording instrument
- Box (shelter) for the equipment
- Small broom
- Snow shovel

Note: In some cases the weather sensors listed above have been linked to data loggers where, in most instances, comparable data may be obtained (see Appendix E). However, a broken wire or power outage may render automated data useless, so manual observations are still preferred as a baseline.

1.7 Field Book Notes

There are many good and different methods for taking field notes. Following these general practices will ensure that quality data are collected (see Figure 1.2 for example).
- Do not leave blanks. If a value was not observed, record N/O for not observed.
- Only write "0" when the reading is zero, for example, when no new snow has accumulated on the new snow board.
- Only record values that are actually observed.

1.8 Field Weather Observations

Heli-ski guiding, ski touring and similar operations often observe general weather conditions in the field. These observations may serve as an interval measurement, accompany a snow profile, or serve to document conditions across a portion of their operational area. The records should describe some of the parameters listed in this section, but field reports should be made as a series of comments so as not to be confused with observations taken at a fixed weather station. Maximum and minimum temperatures cannot be observed but a range in present temperatures can be reported. Field observations should specify the elevation range and the time, or time range, from where the observations were taken. Common field observations typically include: time, location, elevation, sky cover, wind speed and direction, air temperature and precipitation type and rate. Field weather observations that are estimates and not measurements should be recorded with a tilde (~) to denote that the value is approximate.

1.9 Location ✦

Record the location and elevation, or study plot name, at the top of the record book page.

1.10 Date ✦

Record the year, month and day. Avoid spaces, commas etc., i.e. December 5, 2001, is noted as 20011205 (YYYYMMDD). This representation of the date is conducive to automated sorting routines.

1.11 Time ✦

Record the time of observation using a 24-hour clock (avoid spaces, colons etc.) (i.e. 5:10 p.m. is noted as 1710). Use local standard time (i.e. Pacific, Mountain, etc. as appropriate). Operations that overlap time zones should standardize to one time.

1.12 Sky Condition ✦

Classify the amount of cloud cover and record it using the definitions in Table 1.1. Observers may select a separate data code for each cloud layer or one code for the total cloud cover.

Manual Snow and Weather Observations

Table 1.1 Sky Condition

Class	Symbol	Data Code	Definition
Clear	◯	CLR	No Clouds
Few	◔	FEW	Few clouds: up to 2/8 of the sky is covered with clouds
Scattered	◑	SCT	Partially cloudy: 3/8 to 4/8 of the sky is covered with clouds
Broken	◐	BKN	Cloudy: more than half but not all of the sky is covered with clouds (more than 4/8 but less than 8/8 cover)
Overcast	⊕	OVC	Overcast: the sky is completely covered (8/8 cover)
Obscured	⊗	X	A surface based layer (i.e. fog) or a non-cloud layer prevents observer from seeing the sky

Valley Fog/Cloud

Where valley fog or valley cloud exists **below** the observation site, estimate the elevation of the top and bottom of the fog layer in feet (meters) above sea level. Give the elevation to the nearest 100 ft (or 50 m). Data code: VF.

Example: Clear sky with valley fog from 7,500 to 9,000 ft is coded as CLR VF 7500-9000.

Thin Cloud

The amount of cloud, not the opacity, is the primary classification criterion. Thin cloud has minimal opacity, such that the disk of the sun would still be clearly visible through the clouds if they were between the observer and the sun, and shadows would still be cast on the ground. When the sky condition features a thin *scattered*, *broken* or *overcast* cloud layer then precede the symbol with a dash.

Example: A sky completely covered with thin clouds is coded as -OVC.

1.13 Precipitation Type, Rate, and Intensity ✦

The amount of snow, rain, or water equivalent that accumulates during a time period will help forecasters determine the rate and magnitude of the load increase on the snowpack. In this document, *Precipitation Rate* refers to an estimate of the snow or rain rate. *Precipitation Intensity* is a measurement of water equivalent per hour.

Procedure

Precipitation Type

Note the type of precipitation at the time of observation and record using the codes in Table 1.2.

Table 1.2 Precipitation Type

Data Code	Description
NO	No Precipitation
RA	Rain
SN	Snow
RS	Mixed Rain and Snow
GR	Graupel and Hail
ZR	Freezing Rain

Snow, Weather, and Avalanches

Precipitation Rate

Use the descriptors listed in Table 1.3 to describe the precipitation rate at the time of observation. Record the estimated rate with the appropriate data code in Table 1.3.

Table 1.3 Precipitation Rate

Data Code	Description	Rate
Snowfall Rate (this system is open-ended; any appropriate rate may be specified)		
S –1	Very light snowfall	Snow accumulates at a rate of a trace to about 0.5 cm (~ 0.25 in) per hour
S1	Light snowfall	Snow accumulates at a rate of about 1 cm (~ 0.5 in) per hour
S2	Moderate snowfall	Snow accumulates at a rate of about 2 cm (a little less than 1 in) per hour
S5	Heavy snowfall	Snow accumulates at a rate of about 5 cm (~ 2 in) per hour
S10	Very heavy snowfall	Snow accumulates at a rate of about 10 cm (~ 4 in) per hour
Rainfall Rate		
RV	Very light rain	Rain produces no accumulation, regardless of duration
RL	Light rain	Rain accumulates at a rate up to 2.5 mm (0.1 in) of water per hour
RM	Moderate rain	Rain accumulates at a rate between 2.6 to 7.5 mm (0.1 to 0.3 in) of water per hour
RH	Heavy rain	Rain accumulates at a rate of 7.5 mm (0.3 in) of water per hour or more

Precipitation Intensity

Use measurements of rain or the water equivalent of snow to calculate the precipitation intensity with the following equation:

$$PI\left(\frac{mm}{hr}\right) = \frac{water\ content\ of\ precipitation\ (mm)}{duration\ of\ measurement\ period\ (hr)}$$

Record the results with the data code PI and the measured value in millimeters (inches) of water.

Note: PI values are assumed to be in millimeters. Use the symbol " to signify when inches are used

Example: A precipitation intensity of one half inch per hour would be coded as PI0.5".

1.14 Air Temperature ✦

Temperature is measured in degrees Celsius (abbreviated °C) (°F). The standard air temperature should be observed in a shaded location with the thermometer 1.5 m above the ground or snow surface. At a study site, thermometers should be housed in a Stevenson screen and the lower edge of the screen should be 1.2 to 1.4 meters above the ground or snow surface (Figure 1.3).

Procedure

a) Read the maximum thermometer immediately after opening the Stevenson screen.

b) Read the present temperature from the minimum thermometer, and read the minimum temperature from the minimum thermometer last.

c) Read temperature trend and temperature from the thermograph.

At the end of the temperature observation:

d) Remove any snow that might have drifted into or accumulated on top of the screen.

e) Reset the thermometers after the standard observations (refer to Appendix D).

f) If the Stevenson screen is fitted with a height adjustment mechanism ensure that the screen base is in the range of 1.2 to 1.4 m above the snow surface. *[Note: In heavy snow climates where daily access of the site is not always possible, the Stevenson screen may be mounted on top of a (chair) tower to prevent burial. However the height of the screen should be noted in the metadata.]*

g) Check that the screen door still faces north if any adjustments are made.

Note: Read all air temperatures from thermometers to the nearest 0.5 °C (or whole °F).

If there is snow on the thermometer it should be brushed off prior to reading the instrument and noted in the comment section.

1.14.1 Air Temperature Trend

If available, read the air temperature from the thermograph and record to the nearest whole degree. Use an arrow symbol to record the temperature trend shown on the thermograph trace over the preceding three hours.

Table 1.4 Temperature Trend

Symbol	Data Code	Description
↑	RR	Temperature rising rapidly (> 5 degree increase in past 3 hours)
↗	R	Temperature rising (1 to 5 degree increase in past 3 hours)
→	S	Temperature steady (< 1 degree change in past 3 hours)
↘	F	Temperature falling (1 to 5 degree decrease in past 3 hours)
↓	FR	Temperature falling rapidly (> 5 degree decrease in past 3 hours)

Note: Table 1.4 assumes the use of the Celsius temperature scale. Operations that use the Fahrenheit temperature scale should use a threshold of 10-degrees (rather than 5-degrees) for rapid temperature changes.

Snow, Weather, and Avalanches

Location	Never Summer Site #4, 8,300'					
Observer	MA	EL	BS	NW	RP	BK
Date	20030210	20030211	20030212	20030213	20030214	20030215
Time, Type (Std, Int)	0530, S	2330, I	1130, I	1630, S	0530, S	1630, S
Sky	○	⊗	-⊕	OVC	⊕	CLR
Precip Type/Rate	None	S-1	S1	S3	RL	None
Max Temp (°C)	-2.5	-3.0	-3.0	-1.5	1.0	0.0
Min Temp (°C)	-7.0	-6.0	-4.5	-4.0	-4.0	-11.0
Present Temp (°C)	-6.5	-3.0	-4.0	-1.5	0.0	-10.0
Thermograph (°C)	-7	-3	-4	-1	-0	-10
Thermograph Trend	↗	→	↗	↗	→	↘
20 cm Snow Temp (°C)	-10	-6	-5	-4	-4	-6
Relative Humidity (%)	78	86	96	98	100	67
Interval (cm) HIN	0	T	10	12	4	0
Standard (cm) H2D	0	T	10	12	15	0
New (cm) HN24	0	T	10	12	15	14
Storm (cm), C=cleared HST	0	T	10	20	21	19,C
Snow depth (cm) HS	223	222	231	239	241	239
New water (g)	N/O	N/O	33.6	42	67	0
New water (mm)	N/O	N/O	8	10	16	0
Density (kg/m³)	N/O	N/O	80	83	106	0
Rain gauge (mm)	N/O	N/O	N/O	N/O	3	N/O
Precip gauge (mm)	60	60	67	77	82	82
Foot Pen (cm)	35	35	45	50	50	45
Ram Pen (cm)	40	39	47	55	55	48
Surface Form / Size (mm)		PP/0.3	PP/0.3	PP/0.3	WG/0.3	DF/0.3
Wind Speed / Direction	L, E	Calm	M, SE	L, S	L, SW	M, E
Blowing Snow Extent / Dir	None	None	None	M, S	Prev	U
Barometric Pressure (mb)	852	847	817	813	833	843
Pressure Trend	↘	↘	↓	→	↗	→
Comments						

Figure 1.2 An example of a record sheet of a standard observation.

Figure 1.3 Thermograph housed in a Stevenson screen (photograph by Kelly Elder).

1.15 Relative Humidity (RH)

Read the relative humidity to the nearest one percent (1%) from the hygrograph or weather station output.

Note: The accuracy of relative humidity measurements decreases at low temperatures. Furthermore, the accuracy of any mechanical hygrograph is unlikely to be better than five percent (5%) but trends may be important especially at high RH values. Refer to Appendix D for information on exposure issues and relative humidity measurements.

Depending on location, humidity measurements may be more relevant from mid-slope or upper-elevation sites than from valley-bottom sites.

Hygrographs should be calibrated at the beginning of each season, mid season, and after every time the instrument is moved. Calibration is most important when data from multiple instruments are compared with each other. The simplest calibration method is to make a relative humidity measurement near the Stevenson screen with a psychrometer (aspirated or sling). Calibration should be done midday or at a time when the air temperature is relatively stable. Psychrometer measurements are easier to perform when the air temperature is near or above freezing.

1.16 Barometric Pressure at Station

The SI unit for pressure is the pascal (Pa). For reporting weather observations, barometric pressure should be recorded in millibars (1 mb = 1 hPa = 100 Pa, see Appendix B). The recommended English unit for barometric pressure is inches of mercury (inHg). Conversions from other commonly used pressure units to millibars and inches of mercury are listed in Appendix B.

Snow, Weather, and Avalanches

A variety of instruments including barographs, barometers, altimeters, and electronic sensors can be used to obtain a measure of the barometric pressure. Absolute pressures and/or pressure trends are valuable for weather forecasting.

1.16.1 Pressure Trend

Use an arrow symbol to record the pressure tendency as indicated by the change of pressure in the three hours preceding the observation.

Record the change in barometric pressure in the past three hours.

Table 1.5 Pressure Trend

Symbol	Data Code	Description
↑	RR	Pressure rising rapidly (>2 mb rise per hour)
↗	R	Pressure rising (<2 mb rise per hour)
→	S	Pressure steady (<1 mb change in 3 hours)
↘	F	Pressure falling (<2 mb fall per hour)
↓	FR	Pressure falling rapidly (>2 mb fall per hour)

1.17   20 cm Snow Temperature (T20) ✦

Dig into the snow deep enough to allow access to an area 20 cm (or 8 in) below the surface. Cut a shaded wall of the pit smooth and vertical. Shade the snow surface above the area where the sensor will rest in the snow. Cool the thermometer in the snow at the same height, but a different location, at which the measurement will be taken. Insert the thermometer horizontally 20 cm (or 8 in) below the snow surface and allow it to adjust to the temperature of the snowpack. Once the sensor has reached equilibrium, read the thermometer while the sensor is still in the snow.

Record snow temperature to the nearest degree or fraction of a degree based on the accuracy and precision of the thermometer.

1.18   Surface Penetrability (P) ✦

An indication of the snowpack's ability to support a given load and a relative measure of snow available for wind transport can be gained from surface penetrability measurements. There are several common methods for examining surface penetration. Ram penetration is the preferred method of observation because it produces more consistent results than ski or foot penetration. When performing foot or ski penetration on an incline, average the uphill and downhill depths of the track.

Procedure

Ram Penetration (PR)

Let the first section of a standard ram penetrometer (cone diameter 40 mm, apex angle 60° and mass 1 kg) penetrate the snow slowly under its own weight by holding it vertically with the tip touching the snow surface and dropping it. Read the depth of penetration in centimeters.

Foot Penetration (PF)

Step into undisturbed snow and gently put full body weight on one foot. Measure the depth of the footprint to the nearest centimeter (or whole inch) from 0 to 5 cm and thereafter, to the nearest increment of 5 cm (or 2 in).

> Note: The footprint depth varies between observers. It is recommended that all observers working on the same program compare their foot penetration. Observers who consistently produce penetrations more than 10 cm (or 4 in) above or below the average should not record foot penetrations.

Ski Penetration (PS)

Step into undisturbed snow and gently put full body weight on one ski. Measure the depth of the ski track from its centerline to the nearest centimeter (or whole inch) from 0 to 5 cm and thereafter, to the nearest increment of 5 cm (or 2 in).

Note: Ski penetration is sensitive to the weight of the observer and the surface area of the ski.

1.19   Form (F) and Size (E) of Surface Snow

Record the form and size in millimeters of snow grains at the surface using the *International Classification for Seasonal Snow on the Ground*, (Colbeck and others, 1990) basic classification (Table 1.6).

Experienced observers may use the crust subclasses (Table 1.7) to discriminate between various types of surface deposits and crusts (refer to Appendix F for more detailed information about grain forms).

Table 1.6 Basic Classification of Snow on the Ground

Symbol	Basic Classification	Data Code
+	Precipitation Particles (New Snow)	PP
◎	Machine Made Snow	MM
/	Decomposing and Fragmented Particles	DF
●	Rounded Grains (monocrystalline)	RG
□	Faceted Crystals	FC
∧	Depth Hoar	DH
∨	Surface Hoar	SH
○	Melt Forms	MF
▬	Ice Formations	IF

Note: Modifications to Fierz and others, 2009:

> *The use of a subscript "r" modifier is retained to denote rimed grains in the Precipitation Particles (PP) class and its subclasses except for* **gp**, **hl**, **ip**, *and all of Decomposing and Fragmented Particles (DF) class (Example: PP-r).*

> *Subclasses for surface hoar are listed in Appendix F.*

Table 1.7 Surface Deposits and Crusts Subclass

Symbol	Classification	Data Code
∀	Rime	PPrm
=	Rain crust	IFrc
—	Sun crust, Firnspiegel	IFsc
✇	Wind packed	RGwp
◎◎	Melt freeze crust	MFcr

Snow, Weather, and Avalanches

1.20 Height of Snowpack (HS) ✦

The height of the snowpack should be measured at a geographically representative site preferably within 100 meters (or 300 ft) of the weather study plot. A white stake graduated in centimeters (inches) should be placed at the site. It is best to preserve an area with a radius of about 3 m (or 10 ft) around the snow stake for measurements. Ideally the snow in this area is not disturbed during the winter. Try not to walk through the area and leave naturally forming settlement cones and depressions in place.

Procedure

From a distance of about 3 m (or 10 ft) look across the snow surface at the snow stake. Observe the average snow depth between your position and the stake to the nearest centimeter (or 0.5 inch). Try not to disturb the snow around the stake during the course of a winter season.

Note: HS values are measured vertically (i.e. line of plumb).

1.21 Height of New Snow (HN24) ✦

The new snow measurement in the standard morning observation uses a 24-hour interval. Many operations will find it useful to observe snow fall on more than one interval. However, the 24-hour interval snow board should only be used for 24-hour observations. Additional snow boards should be added for additional observations as necessary. It is highly recommended that both 24-hour and Storm intervals be observed by operations that maintain a study plot. Other commonly used intervals appear in the Snow Board Naming Convention Section 1.21.1.

New snow measurements should be made on a snow board (Figure 1.4). The base plate should have minimum dimensions of 40 cm x 40 cm (or 15 in x 15 in), with an attached rod of 1 m (or 3 ft) in length. Larger boards (60 cm x 60 cm) provide more room to make measurements. The base plate and rod should be painted white to reduce the effects of solar heating.

Procedure

Use a ruler graduated in centimeters (or inches) to measure the depth of snow accumulated on the snow board. Take measurements in several spots on the board. Calculate the average of the measurements and record to the nearest cm (in). Record "T" (signifying a trace) when the depth is less than 1 cm (or 0.5 in), or when snow fell but did not accumulate. If there is no new snow record zero. Do not consider surface hoar on the boards as snowfall; clear off hoar layer after observation. If both rain and snow fell it should be noted in the remarks.

The sample on the snow board can also be used to measure the water equivalent of new snow (Section 1.22). Once the observations are complete, redeposit the snow in the depression left by the snow board, adding additional snow if necessary to reposition the board level with the surrounding snow surface.

Note: If the snow board was not level the measurement should be made normal to the surface of the board.

14

1.21.1 Snow Board Naming Conventions

The following convention can be used to identify snow boards used for different interval measurements.

HN24 – 24-hour Board: The HN24 board is used to measure snow that has been deposited over a 24-hour period. It is cleared at the end of the morning standard observation.

HST – Storm Board: Storm snowfall is the depth of snow that has accumulated since the beginning of a storm period. The storm board is cleared at the end of a standard observation prior to the next storm and after useful settlement observations have been obtained. The symbol "C" is appended to the recorded data when the storm board is cleared.

H2D – Twice-a-Day Board: An H2D board is used when standard observations are made twice a day. In this case both the HN24 and H2D boards should be cleared in the morning and then the H2D board is cleared again in the afternoon.

HSB – Shoot Board: The shoot board holds the snow accumulated since the last time avalanches were controlled by explosives. The symbol "C" is appended to the recorded data when the shoot board is cleared.

HIN – Interval Board: An interval board is used to measure the accumulated snow in periods shorter than the time between standard observations. The interval board is cleared at the end of every observation.

HIT – Intermittent Board: Snow boards may be used at sites that are visited on an occasional basis. Snow that accumulates on the board may result from more than one storm. The intermittent snow board is cleared at the end of each observation.

Figure 1.4 a) Snow board graduated in centimeters b) Automated snow board and snow board graduated in inches (photographs by Tom Leonard).

Snow, Weather, and Avalanches

1.22 Water Equivalent of New Snow (HN24W) ✦

The water equivalent is the depth of the layer of water that would form if the snow on the board melted. It is equal to the amount of liquid precipitation. The standard morning observation includes the water equivalent of the new snow on a 24-hour interval. The same snow board used for a 24-hour or other interval measurement should be used to calculate the water equivalent. There are several suitable methods for making this measurement. Three different methods are described in the following section.

Procedure

Use one of the following methods to calculate the water equivalent of the new snow. Record the value to the nearest 0.1 mm (or 0.01 in). Make several measurements and report the average value. Record "T" (signifying a trace) when the snow depth is less than 1 cm (or 0.5 in). If there is no new snow record a zero. Do not consider surface hoar on the boards as snowfall; clear off hoar layer after observation.

Snow Board Tube and Weighing Scale
   a)   Cool the measurement tube in the shade prior to making the measurement
   b)   Hold the tube vertically above the surface of the snow on the snow board
   c)   Press the tube into the snow at a slow and constant rate until it hits the base plate of the snow board
   d)   Record the height of the snow sample in the tube
   e)   Remove the snow next to one side of the tube with a large putty knife or scraper
   f)   Slide putty knife under the tube and remove the sample from the board
   g)   Weigh the sample and read the water content from the scale or use the equation listed below
   h)   Repeat and record the average of several measurements to the nearest 0.1 mm (or 0.01 in)

Melting the Snow Sample
The water equivalent of the new snow can be obtained either by melting a sample of snow and measuring the resulting amount of melt water. The height of the melt water in mm (in) is the water equivalent of the sample. When using this method, the base area of the snow sample and the melted sample much remain the same.

Indirect Method:
The water equivalent of a snow can be obtained weighing a snow sample of known cross-sectional area. Water equivalent is calculated by using the following equation.

$$H2DW\,(mm) = \frac{mass\ of\ snow\ sample\ (g)}{area\ of\ sample\ tube\ (cm^2)} \times 10$$

This method is commonly used by avalanche operations because of its ease (Note: 1 cm³ of water has a mass of 1 g). The expanded equation is in Appendix B, Section B.5.

1.23 Density of New Snow (ρ)

Density is a measure of *mass* per unit *volume*; density is expressed in SI units of kg/m³. It is also common for avalanche operations to discuss snow density in percent water content per volume. Calculations of both quantities are described below. Data records of snow density should be recorded in units of kg/m³. The Greek symbol ρ (rho) is used to represent density.

Calculate density as follows:

Divide the mass (g) of new snow by the sample volume (cm³) and multiply by 1000 to express the result in kilograms per cubic meter (kg/m³). Record as a whole number (i.e. 120 kg/m³).

$$\rho \left(\frac{kg}{m^3} \right) = \frac{mass\ of\ snow\ sample\ (g)}{sample\ volume\ (cm^3)} \times 1000$$

16

For measurements from standard observations:

$$\rho\left(\frac{kg}{m^3}\right) = \frac{H2DW\ (mm)}{H2D\ (cm)} \times 100$$

The water content of a snow sample is often communicated as a dimensionless ratio or percent. Calculate this ratio by dividing the height of the water in a snow layer by the height of the snow layer and then multiply by 100 (e.g. 10 cm of snow that contains 1 cm of water has a water content of 10%).

This ratio can also be calculated by dividing the density of the snow (kg/m^3) by the density of water (1000 kg/m^3) and multiplying by one hundred. Using the density of water allows for an easy calculation by moving the decimal one space to the left (i.e. 80 kg/m^3 = 8%).

$$\%\ water = \frac{water\ equivalent\ of\ snow\ sample\ (mm)}{height\ of\ snow\ sample\ (mm)} \times 100$$

$$\%\ water = \frac{water\ equivalent\ of\ snow\ sample\ (mm)}{height\ of\ snow\ sample\ (cm)} \times 10$$

$$\%\ water = \frac{water\ equivalent\ of\ snow\ sample\ (in)}{height\ of\ snow\ sample\ (in)} \times 100$$

1.24 Rain ✢

There are a variety of commercial rain gauges available. The standard rain gauge is made of metal and has an 8-inch (~20 cm) orifice (Figure 1.5). However, good results can be obtained with commercially manufactured 4-inch (~10 cm) diameter plastic gauges. The gauge should be mounted at the study site (see Appendix D for site guidelines). If a mounted gauge is not available, an 8-inch (~20 cm) gauge may be placed on the snow board prior to a rain event.

Procedure

Measure the amount of rain that has accumulated in the rain gauge with the length scale on the gauge or a ruler. Record the amount to the nearest 0.1 mm (or 0.01 in). Empty the gauge at each standard observation.

Figure 1.5 Precipitation gauge with Alter shield (photograph by Tom Leonard).

Snow, Weather, and Avalanches

1.25 Accumulated Precipitation

Accumulated precipitation gauges collect snowfall, rainfall and other forms of precipitation and continuously record their water equivalent. There are a variety of commercial gauges (both manual and automated) available.

Procedure

Record the amount of precipitation accumulated in the recording precipitation gauge to the nearest tenth of a millimeter (0.1 mm) (or 0.01 of an inch). The amount of precipitation that fell during a single event can be obtained by taking the difference between the present reading and the previous reading.

1.26 Wind ✦

Both *estimates* and *measurements* of wind speed and direction are useful to observe and record. However, it is important to distinguish between the two types of observations. Measurements are made with an instrument located at a fixed point. Estimates are made without instruments or with hand-held instruments, and typically represent wind in a local area rather than at a fixed point.

Procedure

Estimated Wind Speed

For the standard morning observation, an estimate of the wind speed can be obtained by observing for two minutes. Use the indicators in Table 1.8 to determine the categorical wind speed, and the data codes to record average conditions during the observation period.

Estimated Maximum Wind Gust

Estimate the maximum wind speed during the observation period. Record the estimated speed to the nearest 2 m/s (or 5 mi/hr).

Measured Wind Speed

The SI unit for wind speed is meters per second (miles per hour). Refer to Appendix B for unit conversions.

Measured Maximum Wind Gust

Record the speed and time of occurrence of the maximum wind gust.

Table 1.8 Wind Speed Estimation

Class	Data Code	km/h	m/s	mi/h	Typical Indicator
Calm	C	0	0	0	No air motion. Smoke rises vertically.
Light	L	1-25	1-7	1-16	Light to gentle breeze; flags and twigs in motion.
Moderate	M	26-40	8-11	17-25	Fresh breeze; small trees sway. Flags stretched. Snow begins to drift.
Strong	S	41-60	12-17	26-38	Strong breeze; whole trees in motion.
Extreme	X	>60	>17	>38	Gale force or higher.

Note: The indicators used to estimate the wind speed are established by rule of thumb. Observers should develop their own relationships specific to their area.

Wind estimates (speed and direction) should be averaged over a two-minute period prior to the observation.

Since wind speed classes are determined by an estimate, mi/h categories can be rounded to the nearest 5 mi/h.

Manual Snow and Weather Observations

Estimated Wind Direction

During a two-minute period, note the direction **from** which the wind blows. The wind direction can be recorded using the compass directions listed in Table 1.9. Do not record a direction when the wind speed is zero (calm).

Measured Wind Direction

Measured wind direction for standard observations should be rounded to the nearest 10 degrees (i.e. 184 degrees (just beyond south) is coded as 180). Forty-five degrees (northeast) is coded as 050. Archived wind direction data from an automatic weather station can be stored as a three-digit number.

Table 1.9 Wind Direction

Direction	N	NE	E	SE	S	SW	W	NW
Degrees	0	45	90	135	180	225	270	315

1.27   Blowing Snow

Estimate the extent of snow transport (Table 1.10) and note the direction **from** which the wind blows to the closest octant of the compass (Table 1.11). The observer should also note the location and/or elevation of the wind transport (e.g. valley bottom, study site, ridgetop, peaks, 11,000 ft, 3000 m, etc...).

Table 1.10 Extent of Blowing Snow

Data Code	Description
None	No snow transport observed.
Prev	Snow transport has occurred since the last observation but there is no blowing snow activity at the time of observation.
L	Light snow transport.
M	Moderate snow transport.
I	Intense snow transport.
U	Unknown as observation is impossible because of darkness, cloud, or fog.

Record wind direction as indicated by blowing snow.

Table 1.11 Direction of Blowing Snow

Direction	N	NE	E	SE	S	SW	W	NW
Degrees	0	45	90	135	180	225	270	315

Snow, Weather, and Avalanches

Figure 1.6 Wind transport of snow along a mountain ridgeline (photography by Andy Gleason).

Snowpack Observations

2.1 Introduction

Information on the structure and stability of the snowpack within an area is essential to assessing current and future avalanche conditions. In certain applications, starting zones may be inaccessible and snowpack properties can be estimated with careful analysis of past and present weather and avalanche events. Snowpack parameters vary in time and space and observation schemes should address these variations. Snowpack information is generally observed and recorded separately from the snow and weather observations outlined in Chapter 1. However, some basic weather observations are typically made in conjunction with snowpack observations.

Broad objectives are outlined in Section 2.2. A set of standard parameters to be collected with any snowpack observation follows in Section 2.3. Snow profiles and snowpack measurements are described in Sections 2.4 and 2.5. In Section 2.6 methods for observing and recording shear quality are discussed. Section 2.7 presents column and block stability tests, slope cuts are described in Section 2.8, non-standardized tests are described in Section 2.9, and instrumented measures are listed in Section 2.10.

2.2 Objectives

The primary objective of any observer working in avalanche terrain is safety. Secondary objectives may include observing and recording the current structure and stability of the snowpack. Specific measurements and observations may include other objectives that will depend on the type of operation.

Specific measurements and observations will be dependent on the type of operation, but in general the objective is to observe and record the current structure and stability of the snowpack. More specific objectives are listed in the sections that follow.

Figure 2.1 There are many different approaches to observing snowpack properties. (illustration by Sue Ferguson).

Snow, Weather, and Avalanches

2.3   Standard Snowpack Observation

The snowpack parameters observed and the detail of those observations will depend on the particular forecasting problem. This section presents an outline for daily snowpack observations. Parameters one through five and seven will be useful for most avalanche forecasting programs. Individual programs and field workers should select snow properties from those listed in this chapter (parameter six listed below) to supply the information needed for their specific application.

1) *Date* – record the date on which the observation was made (YYYYMMDD).
2) *Time* – record the local time at which the observation was begun (24-hour clock).
3) *Observer* – record the name or names of the personnel that made the observation.
4) *Site Characteristics*
    a. *Observation Location-* record the nearest prominent topographic landmark (mountain, pass, drainage, avalanche path, etc.), political landmark (town, road mile, etc.), or geographic coordinates (latitude/longitude or UTM). If observing a fracture line profile, note the location within the avalanche path.
    b. *Aspect* – record the direction that the slope faces where the observation was made (i.e. N, NE, E, SE, S, SW, W, NW, or degrees azimuth).
    c. *Elevation* – record the elevation of the observation site in feet (meters).
    d. *Slope Angle* – record the incline of the slope where the observation was made (degrees).
5) *Current Weather*
    a. *Sky Conditions-* record the sky conditions as Clear, Few, Scattered, Broken, Overcast, or Obscured (Section 1.12).
    b. *Air temperature* – record the current air temperature to the nearest 0.5 °C (or whole °F).
    c. *Precipitation Type and Rate* – record the precipitation type and rate using the scale and data codes in Section 1.13.
    d. *Wind* – record the wind speed and direction (Section 1.26)
    e. *Surface Penetration* – record the surface penetration using one of the methods described in Section 1.18.
6) *Snowpack Properties* – observe and record the necessary snowpack properties as described in this chapter.
7) *Avalanche Potential* – record one or more of the parameters as applicable to the operation (see Appendix G). Avalanche conditions can be grouped by region, aspect, slope angle range (i.e. 35°-40°), or obvious snow properties (such as recently wind loaded or amount of new snow). In this case a separate stability, danger, or hazard rating should be given for each group.
    a. *Snow Stability*
        i. *Forecast* – record the snow stability stated in the morning meeting or current forecast.
        ii. *Observed* – record the snow stability observed at this location
    b. *Avalanche Danger*
        i. *Forecast* – record the avalanche danger stated in the current avalanche advisory.
        ii. *Observed* – record the avalanche danger observed at this location
    c. *Avalanche Hazard*
        i. *Forecast* – record the avalanche hazard currently stated by the program
        ii. *Observed* – record the avalanche hazard observed at this location.

2.4 Snow Profiles

Snow profiles are observed at *study plots, study slopes, fracture lines* and *targeted sites*. This section outlines two types of snow profiles: *full profiles* and *test profiles*. A full profile is a complete record of snow-cover stratigraphy and characteristics of individual layers. A test profile is a record of selected observations.

Full Profiles

Full snow profiles are frequently observed at study plots or study slopes in time series to track changes in the snowpack. They require that all, or most, snowpack variables be measured (Section 2.5). Full profiles are time consuming and not always possible at targeted sites.

Test Profiles

Test profiles are the most common type of snow profile. There is no fixed rule about the type and amount of information collected in a test profile. Each observer must select, observe and record the parameters needed by their operation. These parameters may change in both time and space. Test profiles are commonly observed at targeted sites and fracture lines.

Figure 2.2 Different types of snow profiles: a) Full Profile, b) Test Profile c) Fracture Line Profile. Snow profiles will vary depending the information needed to support a particular application (photographs by Mount Shasta Avalanche Center (a), Bruce Tremper (b), and Ben Pritchett (c)).

The objectives of observing *full profiles* are to:

   a) Identify the layers of the snowpack
   b) Identify the hardness and/or density of the layers in the snowpack
   c) Identify weak interfaces between layers and to approximate their stability
   d) Observe snow temperatures
   e) Monitor and confirm changes in snowpack stability
   f) Determine the thickness of a potential slab avalanche
   g) Determine the state of metamorphism in different snow layers
   h) Observe and record temporal and spatial changes in snow properties

A *test profile* would address one or more of the above objectives.

In addition, this information can be used for climatalogical studies, forecasts of snow-melt runoff, engineering applications, and studies of the effect of snow on vegetation and wildlife.

Typical Full Profile
A typical full profile may include the following observations:

- Total Depth
- Temperature by depth (Section 2.5.1)
- Identification of layer boundaries (Section 2.5.2)
- Density of each layer (Section 2.5.7)
- Water content of each layer (Section 2.5.6)
- Hand hardness of each layer (Section 2.5.3)
- Grain type and size of each layer (Sections 2.5.4 and 2.5.5)
- Stability tests (Sections 2.6, 2.7, 2.9, and 2.10)
- Comments

2.4.1   Location
Snow profiles can be observed at a variety of locations depending on the type of information desired. Typical locations include study plots, study slopes, fracture lines, or targeted sites. Full profiles are usually conducted at study plots, study slopes, and fracture lines, however full profiles and test profiles can be completed at any location.

Study Plot
Study plots are used to observe and record parameters for a long-term record. They are fixed locations that are carefully chosen to minimize contamination of the observations by external forces such as wind, solar radiation, slope angle, and human activity (See Appendix D). Study plots are typically flat sites and can be co-located with a meteorological observing station.

Observations are carried out at a study plot by excavating each snow pit progressively in a line marked with two poles. Subsequent observation pits should be at a distance about equal to the total snow depth, but at least 1 m from the previous one. After each observation, the extreme edge of the pit is marked with a pole to indicate where to dig the next pit (i.e. at least 1 m from that point). When the observations are complete, the snowpit should be refilled with snow to minimize atmospheric influences on lower snowpack layers.

Study plots and study slopes should be selected and marked before the winter and the ground between the marker poles cleared of brush and large rocks. Some operations will require multiple study plots to adequately track snowpack conditions.

Study Slope
The best snow stability information is obtained from snow profiles observed in avalanche starting zones. Since starting zones are not always safely accessible, other slopes can be selected that are reasonably representative of individual or a series of starting zones. Choosing a safe location for a study slope is

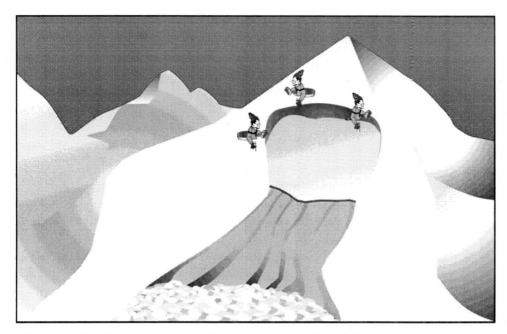

Figure 2.3 Possible locations for a fracture line profile. From left to right: undisturbed snow in the flank, undisturbed snow in the crown, on the crown face.

critical. The study slope should be relatively uniform in aspect and slope angle, and with the exception of the observations should remain undisturbed during the winter. The study slope may be pre-selected and marked in the same manner as study plots; however, marker poles on slopes will be tilted by snow creep and may have to be periodically reset. Some operations may find it advantageous to collect their time series observations on a study slope in addition to, or in place of, a study plot. Multiple study slopes may be useful.

Fracture Line

Observing snow profiles near an avalanche fracture line can provide valuable information about the cause of the slide. Safety considerations are paramount when selecting a site for a profile. Before approaching a site, observers must evaluate the potential for and consequences of further releases. Snow profiles can be observed on a crown face or flank as well as areas where the weak layer did not fracture. When possible, profiles should be observed at a fracture line and at least 1.5 m away from the crown face or flank in undisturbed snow.

Fracture line profiles should be observed at as many locations as possible, including thick and thin sections of the fracture line. In addition, use a sketch or camera to document the location of prominent features and location of fracture line profiles. Carefully note terrain, vegetation, solar, and wind effects on the snowpack. Note any evidence of past avalanche activity which may have influenced the structure of the snowpack.

> *Note: The snow that remains following an avalanche can be either stronger than what slid or dangerously weak. Care should also be taken to choose a location where average crown depth is not exceeded. It is preferable to examine the snow along a fracture line at as many places as possible as time allows.*

Figure 2.4 A targeted site for a snow profile (photograph by Doug Richmond).

Targeted Site

A targeted site is selected to satisfy a particular observer's objectives. The site should be selected to target parameters of interest. Keep in mind that exposure to wind, solar radiation, elevation, and other factors produce variations in snowpack characteristics.

General rules for choosing a targeted site include:

- Always evaluate the safety of a location prior to observing a snow profile.
- To minimize the effects of trees, dig the snow pit no closer to trees than the height of the nearest tree (draw an imaginary line from the top of the tree at a 45 degree angle to the snow surface). In high traffic areas, or when evaluating forested slopes this criterion may not be practical.
- Avoid depressions such as gullies or other terrain traps.
- Avoid heavily compacted areas such as tree wells, canopy sluffs, and tracks made by humans or other animals.

2.4.2 Frequency of Observations

No firm rules can be set on how frequently snow profiles should be observed. Frequency is dependent on climate, terrain, access to starting zones, recent weather, current snow stability, type of avalanche operation, and other considerations. Full profiles should be conducted at regular intervals at study plots and study slopes. Profiles at fracture lines and targeted sites can be completed on an as-needed basis.

2.4.3   Equipment
The following equipment can be useful when observing snow profiles:

> a) Probe
> b) Snow shovel (flat bladed shovels are preferred)
> c) Snow thermometer (calibrated regularly)
> d) Ruler or probe graduated in centimeters
> e) Magnifying glass (5x or greater)
> f) Crystal card
> g) Field book
> h) Two pencils
> i) Gloves
> j) Snow saw
> k) Inclinometer
> l) Compass (adjusted for declination)
> m) Density kit
> n) Brush
> o) Altimeter (calibrated regularly)
> p) Topographic map
> q) Global positioning system (GPS)

The thermometers should be calibrated periodically in a slush mixture after the free water has been drained. Glass thermometers must be checked for breaks in the mercury or alcohol columns before every use.

2.4.4   Field Procedure
Equipment
Equipment used to measure or observe snow properties should be kept in the shade and/or cooled in the snow prior to use.

Observers should wear gloves to reduce thermal contamination of measurements.

Checking Snow Depth
Check the snow depth with a probe before digging the observation pit and make sure the pit is not on top of a boulder, bush or in a depression. Careful probing can also be used to obtain a first indication of snow layering. Probing prior to digging is not necessary in a study plot, or when the snow is much deeper than your probe.

Digging the Snow Pit
Make the hole wide enough to facilitate all necessary observations and to allow shoveling at the bottom. Remember to examine the snow as you dig the pit as valuable information can be obtained during this process. In snow deeper than 2 m it may be advantageous to dig first to a depth of about 1.5 m, make the observations (such as stability tests) and then complete excavation and observations to the necessary depth. The pit face on which the snow is to be observed should be in the shade. Cut the observation face in an adjacent sidewall vertical and smooth. On inclined terrain it is advantageous to make the observations on a shaded sidewall, that is parallel to the fall line

Recording
If there are two observers, the first observer can prepare the pit, while the second observer begins the observations (see Figures 2.7 and 2.8 for examples of field notes):

> a)   Record date, time, names of observers, location, elevation, aspect, slope angle, sky condition, precipitation, wind surface penetrability (foot and ski penetration), and total snow depth.

b) Observe the air temperature to the nearest 0.5 degree in the shade about 1.5 m above the snow surface. Use a dry thermometer, wait several minutes, and then make several readings about a minute apart to see if the thermometer has stabilized. Record the temperature if there is no change between the two or more readings.

c) Convention for seasonal snow covers is to locate the zero point on the height scale at the ground. However, when the snow cover is deeper than about 3 m it is convenient to locate the zero point at the snow surface. Setting 0 at the snow surface, for test pits, eases comparisons with other snowpack observations made throughout the period. Observers should use whichever protocol fits their needs. In either case the total depth of the snowpack should be recorded when possible.

2.5   Snowpack Observations
2.5.1   Snowpack Temperature (T)

Observe snow temperature to the nearest fraction of a degree based on the accuracy and precision of the thermometers. Most field thermometers can measure snow temperature within 0.5 °C.

Measure the snow surface temperature by placing the thermometer on the snow surface; shade the thermometer.

The temperature profile should be observed as soon as practical after the pit has been excavated.

Push the thermometer horizontally to its full length parallel to the surface into the snow (use the shaded side-wall of the pit on a slope). Wait at least one minute, re-insert close by and then read the temperature while the thermometer is still in the snow. Shade the thermometer in order to reduce influence of radiation. One method is to push the handle of a shovel into the snow surface so that the blade casts a shadow on the snow surface above the thermometer. Shading the snow above your thermometer is important when you are making temperature measurements in the upper 30 cm of the snowpack.

Measure the first sub-surface snow temperature 10 cm below the surface. The second temperature is observed at the next multiple of 10 cm from the previous measurement and from there in intervals of 10 cm to a depth of 1.4 m below the surface, and at 20-cm intervals below 1.4 m. Measure the snow temperatures at closer intervals when needed, as may be the case when the temperature gradients are strong, significant density variations exist, or when the temperatures are near to 0 °C. When measuring relatively small temperature variations, as is common around a crust or density discontinuity, greater accuracy and reliability in measurements may be possible by using a single thermometer/temperature probe.

Begin the next observation while snow temperatures are being measured.

Note: Compare thermometers first when two or more are used simultaneously. Place side-by-side in a homogenous snow layer and compare the measurements. If they do not agree, only one of the thermometers should be used.

Punch a hole in the snowpack with the metal case or a knife before inserting the thermometer into very hard snow and at ground surface.

It is important to regularly check the accuracy of all thermometers by immersing them in a slush mixture after the free water has been drained; each should read 0 °C. Prepare this mixture in a thermos and recalibrate or note variation from 0 °C on the thermometer.

2.5.2   Layer Boundaries

Determine the location of each major layer boundary. Brushing the pit wall with a crystal card or a soft bristle paint brush will help to bring out the natural layering of the snowpack. Identify weak layers or interfaces of layers where a failure might occur. Record the distance from the layer boundary to the ground or snow surface depending on the convention being used.

Figure 2.5 The layered nature of a seasonal snow cover (photograph by Bruce Tremper).

Many operations find it useful to track specific features within the snowpack. Persistent weak layers or layers that are likely to produce significant avalanche activity (such as crusts, surface hoar, or near-surface facts) can be named with the date that they were buried. Some operations also find it useful to number each significant precipitation event and reference potential weak layers with these numbers or as interfaces between two numbered events.

2.5.3 Snow Hardness (R)

Observe the hardness of each layer with the hand hardness test. Record under "R" (resistance) the object that can be pushed into the snow with moderate effort parallel to the layer boundaries.

> *Note: Fierz and others (2009) suggests a maximum force of 10 to 15 newtons (1 to 1.5 kg-force or about 2 or 3 pounds) to push the described object into the snow.*

> *Wear gloves when conducting hand hardness observations.*

Slight variations in hand hardness can be recorded using + and - qualifiers (i.e. P+, P, P-). A value of 4F+ is less hard than 1F-. Individual layers may contain a gradual change in hand hardness value. These variations can be recorded in a graphical format (Figures 2.8 and 2.9), or by using an arrow to point from the upper value to the lower value (i.e. a layer that is soft on top and gets harder as you move down would read 4F+ → 1F).

Table 2.1 Hand Hardness Index

Symbol	Hand Test	Term	Graphic Symbol
F	Fist in glove	Very low	
4F	Four fingers in glove	Low	/
1F	One finger in glove	Medium	X
P	Blunt end of pencil	High	//
K	Knife blade	Very high	※
I	Too hard to insert knife	Ice	■
N/O	Not observed		N/A

2.5.4 Grain Form (F)

The International Classification for Seasonal Snow on the Ground (Fierz and others, 2009) presents a basic classification scheme based on grain morphology and formation process. This scheme is used throughout this document. Primary classes are listed in the table below. Subclasses are listed in Appendix F.

Table 2.2 Basic Classification of Snow on the Ground

Symbol	Basic Classification	Data Code
+	Precipitation Particles (New Snow)	PP
◎	Machine Made snow	MM
/	Decomposing and Fragmented Particles	DF
●	Rounded Grains	RG
□	Faceted Crystals	FC
∧	Depth Hoar	DH
∨	Surface Hoar	SH
○	Melt Forms	MF
■	Ice Formations	IF

Note: Modifications to Fierz and others, 2009:

*The use of a subscript "r" modifier is retained to denote rimed grains in the Precipitation Particles (PP) class and its subclasses except for **gp**, **hl**, **ip**, and all of Decomposing and Fragmented Particles (DF) class (Example: PP-r).*

Subclasses for surface hoar are listed in Appendix F.

Any basic group may be sub-classified into different forms of solid precipitation according to the *International Classification for Seasonal Snow on the Ground*. Commonly, the Precipitation Particles class (graphic symbol "+") may be replaced by one of the following symbols. Snow layers often contain crystals from more than one class or that are in transition between classes. In this case the observer can select primary and secondary classes for a single layer and place the secondary class in parentheses (e.g. a new snow layer composed of mostly plates with some needles could be listed as ⊙ (↔)).

Table 2.3 Basic Classification of snow in the Atmosphere

Symbol	Description	Data Code
□	Columns	PPco
↔	Needles	PPnd
⊙	Plates	PPpl
*	Stellars and dendrites	PPsd
⌒	Irregular crystals	PPir
⋏	Graupel	PPgp
▲	Hail	PPhl
⌂	Ice pellets	PPip

In warm weather the crystals may melt and their shape may change rapidly on the crystal card. In this case, a quick decision must be made and repeated samples taken from various depths of the same layer.

Snow layers often contain crystals in different stages of metamorphism. The classification should refer to the predominant type, but may be mixed when different types are present in relatively equal numbers. A maximum of two grain forms may be displayed for any single layer. The sub-classification in Fierz, and others, 2009 has "mixed forms" classes that can be used by experienced observers who recognize grains that are in a transition stage between classes.

Illustrations of the various types of crystal shapes may be found in the following publications: LaChapelle, 1992; Perla, 1978; Colbeck and others, 1990; McClung and Schaerer, 2006, and Fierz and others 2009.

Refer to the *International Classification for Seasonal Snow on the Ground* (Fierz and others, 2009) for complete descriptions of the grain forms listed here.

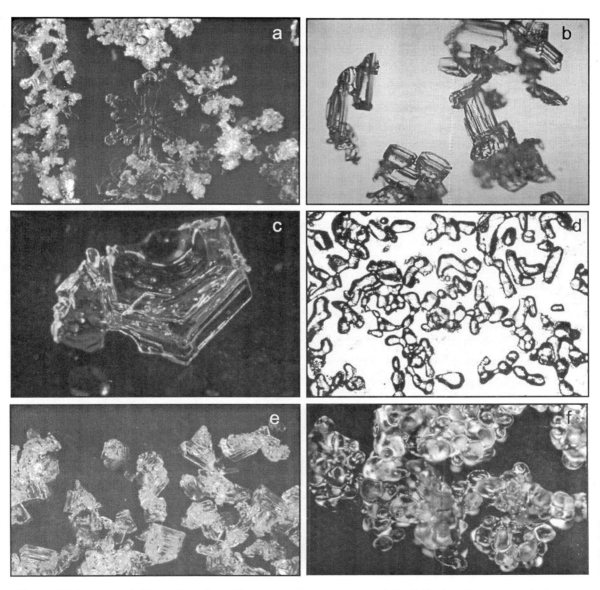

Figure 2.6 Snow crystal formations found in seasonal snow covers. a) Partially rimed new snow (+), b) Faceted grains formed near the snow surface (▨), c) Advanced faceted depth hoar (∧) d) Rounded snow grains (•), e) Faceted snow grains (□), , f) Clustered melt forms (⊽) (photographs by Kelly Elder (a,c), Joe Stock (b), courtesy of John Montagne (d), Ethan Greene (e), and Sam Colbeck (f)).

2.5.5 Grain Size (E)

Determine the grain size in each layer with the aid of a crystal card. In doing so, disregard the small particles and determine the average **greatest extension** of the grains that make up the bulk of the snow. Record the size or the range of sizes in millimeters in column "E". Record size to the nearest 0.5 mm, except for fine and very fine grains which may be recorded as 0.1, 0.3 or 0.5mm.

Where two distinct grain forms exist in a layer, list the size of the primary crystal form first followed by the size of the secondary class in parentheses.

Example: 0.3 (2.5)

Where a range in sizes exists for any single grain form, specify the average and maximum size with a hyphen.

Example: 0.5-1.5

The above notations can also be combined.

Example: 0.5-1.0 (2.5)

2.5.6 Liquid Water Content (θ)

Classify liquid water content by volume of each snow layer that has a temperature of 0 °C. Gently squeeze a sample of snow with a gloved hand and observe the reaction; record in the column headed "θ" (theta).

Table 2.4 Liquid Water Content of Snow (adapted from Fierz and others, 2009)

Class	Definition	Water Content (by volume)	Symbol	Data Code
Dry	Usually the snow temperature (T) is below 0 °C but dry snow can occur at any temperature up to 0 °C. Disaggregated snow grains have little tendency to adhere to each other when pressed together. Difficult to make a snowball.	0 %		D
Moist	T = 0 °C. Water is not visible even at 10 x magnification. When lightly crushed, the snow has a distinct tendency to stick together. Snowballs are easily made.	<3 %			M
Wet	T = 0 °C. Water can be recognized at 10x magnification by its meniscus between adjacent snow grains, but water cannot be pressed out by moderately squeezing the snow in the hands (Pendular regime).	3 - 8 %	||	W
Very Wet	T = 0 °C. Water can be pressed out by moderately squeezing the snow by hand, but there is some air confined within the pores (Funicular regime)	8 – 15%	|||	V
Slush	T = 0 °C. The snow is flooded with water and contains a relatively small amount of air.	>15%	||||	S

2.5.7 Density (ρ)

Measure density of the snow in layers that are thick enough to allow insertion of the snow sampling device. Small samplers are more suitable for measuring the density of thin layers and larger samplers are better suited for depth hoar.

Insert the sample cutter into the pit wall, compacting the sample as little as possible. On angled slopes, sampling on the pit sidewall will make it easier to sample a single layer. Samples used for bulk density calculations can contain more than one snow layer, otherwise be sure to sample one layer if possible. Trim the excess snow off the cutter and weigh. Either write down the mass under comments and calculate density later, or calculate density on site and note it in the column headed "ρ" (rho).

Calculate density as follows: Divide the mass (g) of the snow sample by the sample volume (cm^3) and multiply by 1000 to express the result in kg/m^3. Record as a whole number.

$$\rho\left(\frac{\text{kg}}{\text{m}^3}\right) = \frac{\text{mass of snow sample (g)}}{\text{sample volume (cm}^3\text{)}} \times 1000$$

Practical methods for calculating snow density can be established based on the snow volume sampled. For example, when using a 500 cm^3 snow sampling tube multiply the mass of snow sample in the tube by 2, with a 250 cm^3 sampler, multiply the snow sample mass by 4, etc.

2.5.8 Strength and Stability Tests

Perform tests of strength and stability as appropriate (see Sections 2.6, 2.7, 2.9, and 2.10 for details on individual tests). It may be advantageous to perform multiple tests or iterations of a test.

2.5.9 Marking the Site

If additional observations are to be made at this site, fill the pit and place a marker pole at the extreme edge. Pits dug in areas open to the public should be filled back in with snow.

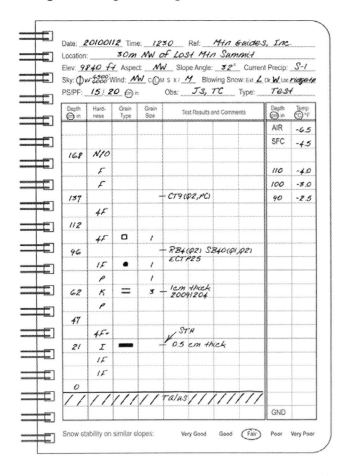

Figure 2.7 Example of field notes from a test profile.

Snow, Weather, and Avalanches

2.5.10 Graphical Snow Profile Representation

Snow profiles can be represented graphically in a standard format for quick reference and permanent record (Figures 2.8 and 2.9).

a) Plot the snow temperatures as a curve; mark the air temperature above the snow surface and use a dashed line to connect the two.

b) Plot the height of the snow layers to scale.

c) Use graphic symbols for the shape of grains and liquid water content. Record N/O when the hardness or liquid water content can not be determined (a blank implies fist hardness or dry snow respectively). *Use of graphic symbols for hardness is optional.*

d) Tabulate grain size and density with the values observed in the field.

e) Include written comments where appropriate. If possible, label important layers by their date of burial.

f) Include the results of appropriate strength and stability tests in the comments column.

g) Document grain form and size of the failure layer. Draw an arrow at the height of each observed failure and use a shorthand notation to describe the test. When multiple tests are performed the results of every test should be included.

Examples:

STE (Q1) SH 2.5 (shovel shear test, easy shear, quality 1, on 2.5 mm surface hoar)

RB6 (Q2) FC 1.5 (rutschblock score six, quality 2, on 1.5 mm faceted crystals)

CT8 (Q1) DH 2.0 (compression test, on 8th tap, quality 1, on 2.0 mm depth hoar)

CT12 (Q1x2) ⍒ (two compression tests on 12th tap, quality 1, on graupel)

SB30 (Q2,Q2) □ (two stuff block tests both 30 cm drop, quality 2, faceted grains)

SB20, 30 (Q2) (two stuff block tests, one on 20 cm drop, one on 30 cm drop, both quality 2)

h) Plot the hand hardness test results as a horizontal bar graph (Figures 2.8 and 2.9). If a snowpack layer has variable hand hardness, the length of the upper or lower ends of the bar can be shortened or lengthened and the connecting line angled or curved to reflect the variation (Figures 2.8 and 2.9). Changes in hardness category can be emphasized by using the bar lengths in Table 2.5. In regions where both weak layers and slabs are composed of very soft snow (1F or softer), it may be beneficial to plot the hard hardness index using the same distance to represent each category.

Table 2.5 Graphical Representation of Hand Hardness Index

Object in Hand Test	Length of Bar (mm)
Fist in glove	5
Four fingers in glove	10
One finger in glove	20
Blunt end of pencil	40
Knife blade	80
Ice	100

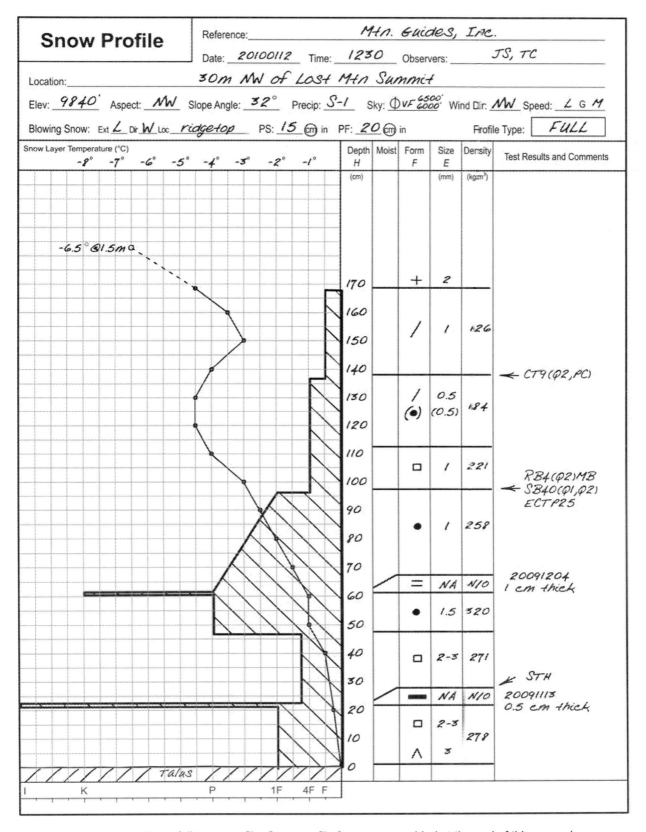

Figure 2.8 Hand drawn full snow profile. Snow profile forms are provided at the end of this manual.

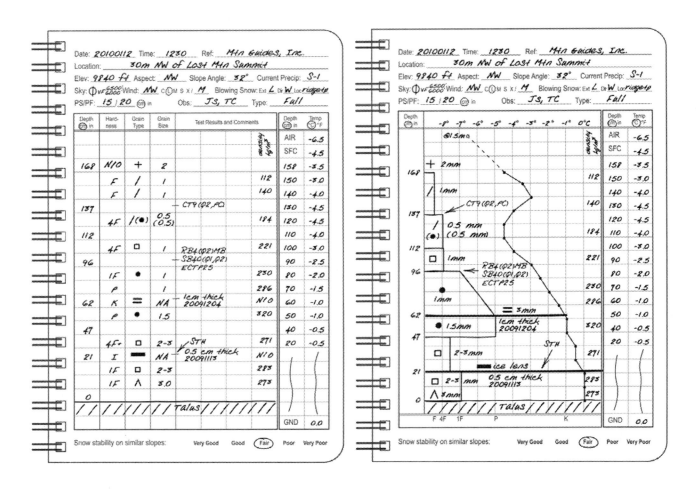

Figure 2.9 Two different methods for recording field notes from a full profile.

2.6 Characterizing Fractures in Column and Block Tests

Many of the stability tests described in the following sections yield some indication of the load required to produce a fracture. In addition to the magnitude of the load, observing the nature of the fracture can improve estimations of snow stability and can, in particular, reduce false-stable results (Johnson and Birkeland, 1998; Birkeland and Johnson, 1999; Johnson and Birkeland 2002; Birkeland and Johnson 2003; van Herwijnen and Jamieson, 2004; van Herwijnen, 2005). Both methods described below can be included with the results of a column or block test (see Section 2.7.3) and provide additional information about the stability of the snow slope. All the research with these methods has been conducted using compression-type tests such as the compression, stuffblock and rutschblock tests.

Snowpack Observations

The methods described in this section provide a qualitative assessment of the fracture propagation potential. Although the definitions and approach differ, the phenomenon they describe are essentially identical (Table 2.6). Both methods require experienced observers to make somewhat subjective assessments, especially when trying to determine whether a planar fracture is sudden (SP/Q1) or resistant (RP/Q2). Members of an operational program should select the method that works best for their application and periodically calibrate their ratings to ensure consistency.

Table 2.6 A comparison of the categories in the Fracture Character and Shear Quality scales (after van Herwijnen and Jamieson, 2003 and Birkeland, 2004).

Fracture Character Category	Fracture Character Data Code		Typical Shear Quality
	Subclass	Major class	
Sudden planar	SP	SDN	Q1
Sudden collapse	SC		
Resistant planar	RP		Q2
		RES	
Progressive compression	PC		Q2 or Q3
Break	BRK	BRK	Q3

2.6.1 Shear Quality

Shear Quality was developed by avalanche workers at the Gallatin National Forest Avalanche Center (southwest Montana). It can be used with any of the stability tests in this chapter, but was developed primarily for use with the rutschblock, compression, and stuffblock tests.

Procedure
a) Conduct any of the stability tests described in this chapter.
b) Carefully observe how the fracture occurs and examine the nature of the fracture plane.
c) Record the results in accordance with the shear quality definitions (Table 2.7).

Recording
The results can be included at the end of any shear test result. Example: A rutschblock score of 2 with a shear quality of 1 would be recorded as RB2(Q1). A compression test that fractured with 5 taps from the elbow producing a rough shear plane would be recorded as CT15(Q3). A stuffblock test that fractured on the static loading step and produced a moderately clean shear would be recorded as SB0(Q2).

Snow, Weather, and Avalanches

Table 2.7 Shear Quality Ratings

Description	Data Code
Unusually clean, planar, smooth and fast shear surface; weak layer may collapse during fracture. The slab typically slides easily into the snow pit after weak layer fracture on slopes steeper than 35 degrees and sometimes on slopes as gentle as 25 degrees. Tests with thick, collapsible weak layers may exhibit a rougher shear surface due to erosion of basal layers as the upper block slides off, but the initial fracture was still fast and mostly planar.	Q1
"Average" shear; shear surface appears mostly smooth, but slab does not slide as readily as Q1. Shear surface may have some small irregularities, but not as irregular as Q3. Shear fracture occurs throughout the whole slab/weak layer interface being tested. The entire slab typically does not slide into the snow pit.	Q2
Shear surface is non-planar, uneven, irregular and rough. Shear fracture typically does not occur through the whole slab/weak layer interface being tested. After the weak layer fractures the slab moves little, or may not move at all, even on slopes steeper than 35 degrees.	Q3

2.6.2 Fracture Character

Fracture Character was developed by the Applied Snow and Avalanche Research group at the University of Calgary. It can be used with any of the stability tests in this chapter and other tests that load a small column of snow until a fracture appears.

Fracture character is best observed in tests performed on a small isolated column of snow where the objective is to load the column until a fracture (or no fracture) occurs. The front face and side walls of the test column should be as smooth as possible. The observer should be positioned in such a way that one side wall and the entire front face of the test column can be observed. Attention should be focused on weak layers or interfaces identified in a profile or previous snowpack.

Procedure

a) Conduct any of the stability tests described in this chapter.

b) Carefully observe how the fracture occurs in the target weak layer. For tests on low-angled terrain that produced planar fractures, it may be useful to slide the two fracture surfaces across one another by carefully grasping the two sides of the block and pulling while noting the resistance.

c) Record the results in accordance with the definitions in Table 2.8.

Recording

The results can be included at the end of any stability test result. Example: A sudden fracture in a rutschblock test with a score of 2 would be recorded as RB2(SDN). A compression test that fractured with 5 taps from the elbow producing a resistant planar fracture would be recorded as CT15(RP). A stuffblock test that fractured on the static loading step and produced a sudden collapse would be recorded as SB0(SC).

Snowpack Observations

Table 2.8 Fracture Character Ratings

Fracture Characteristics	Subclass	Data Code	Major Class	Data Code
A thin planar* fracture suddenly crosses column in one loading step AND the block slides easily** on the weak layer.	Sudden planar	SP	Sudden	SDN
Fracture crosses the column with a single loading step and is associated with a noticeable collapse of the weak layer.	Sudden collapse	SC	Sudden	SDN
A fracture of noticeable thickness (non-planar fractures often greater than 1cm), which usually crosses the column with a single loading step, followed by step-by-step compression of the layer with subsequent loading steps.	Progressive compression	PC	Resistant	RES
Planar or mostly planar fracture that requires more than one loading step to cross column and/or the block does NOT slide easily** on the weak layer.	Resistant planar	RP	Resistant	RES

2.7 Column and Block Tests

2.7.1 Site Selection

Test sites should be safe, geographically representative of the avalanche terrain under consideration, and undisturbed. For example, to gain information about a wind-loaded slope, find a safe part of a similarly loaded slope for the test. The site should not contain buried ski tracks or avalanche deposits. In general, the site should be further than about one tree length from trees where buried layers might be disturbed by wind action or by clumps of snow which have fallen from nearby trees (imagine a line drawn between a tree top and the snow surface, the acute angle between that line and the horizontal should be at most 45°). Föhn (1987a) recommends slope angles of at least 30° for rutschblock tests, but stability tests done on 25° - 30° slopes can yield some useful information. Be aware that near the top of a slope, snowpack layering and hence test scores may differ from the slope below.

Recently, interest in understanding and documenting spatial variations in the physical properties of snow has increased in both the research and applied communities (Schweizer et al. 2008). The general guidelines outlined in the paragraph above remain part of good field practice. However, there is increasing evidence that making more observations is an effective strategy for avalanche operations and can help minimize the frequency of false-stable situations (Birkeland and Chabot, 2006). Both scientists and field workers should maintain a high level of curiosity and continue to search for signs and areas of instability, even during periods when the snow appears to be stable.

2.7.2 Shovel Shear Test

Objective

The shovel shear test provides:

a) information about the location where the snow could fail in a shear; and
b) a qualitative assessment of weak layer strength. It is best applied to identify buried weak layers, and it does not usually produce useful results in layers close to the snow surface.

Equipment

A shovel is the only equipment required for the Shovel Shear Test. However, a snow saw will make cutting the snow column easier and more precise.

Note: Observers are cautioned that identification of the location of weak layers is the primary objective of the shovel shear test. The ratings of effort are subjective and depend on the strength and stiffness of the slab, dimensions of the shovel blade and handle, and the force applied by the tester.

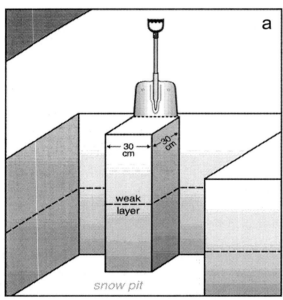

Figure 2.10 a) Schematic and b) photograph of the shovel shear test (photograph by Kelly Elder).

Snowpack Observations

Procedure

a) Expose a fresh pit wall by cutting back about 0.2 m from the wall of a full snow profile or test profile.

b) Observers can remove very soft snow (fist hardness) from the surface of the area where the test is to be carried out if necessary.

c) On the snow surface mark a cross section of the column to be cut, measuring 30 cm wide and 30 cm in the upslope direction (approximately the width of the shovel blade to be used).

d) Cut a chimney wide enough to allow the insertion of the saw on one side of the column and a narrow cut on the other side.

e) Make a vertical cut at the back of the column and leave the cutting tool (saw) at the bottom for depth identification. The back-cut should be 0.7 m deep maximum and end in medium hard to hard snow if possible.

f) Carefully insert the shovel into the back-cut no farther than the heel of the shovel. Hold the shovel handle with both hands and apply an even force in the down-slope (slope parallel) direction. Be careful not to pry the column away from the snow pit wall.

g) When the column breaks in a smooth shear plane above the low end of the back-cut, mark the level of the shear plane on the rear (standing) wall of the back-cut.

h) After a failure in a smooth shear layer or an irregular surface at the low end of the back-cut, or when no failure occurs, remove the column above the bottom of the back-cut and repeat steps e) to g) on the remaining column below.

i) Repeat the test on a second column with the edge of the shovel 0.1 m to 0.2 m above the suspected weak layer.

j) Measure and record the depth of the shear planes if they were equal in both tests. Repeat steps c) to h) if the shear planes were not at the same depth in both tests.

k) If no break occurs, tilt the column and tap (see Section 2.9.4).

l) Use Table 2.7 to classify the results of the test.

m) Observe and classify the crystal shape and size at the shear planes. (Often a sample of the crystals is best obtained from the underside of the sheared block.)

i) Record the results of the test with the appropriate data code from Table 2.9 along with the shear quality, height, and grain type and size of the weak layer (i.e. "STE@125cm↑□ 1mm" would be an easy shear on a layer of 1 mm faceted grains 125 cm above the ground).

Table 2.9 Loading Steps and Shovel Shear Test Scores

Term	Description	Equivalent Shear Strength (Pa)	Data Code
Collapse	Block collapses when cut		STC
Very Easy	Fails during cutting or insertion of shovel	<100	STV
Easy	Fails with minimum pressure	100 – 1000	STE
Moderate	Fails with moderate pressure	1000 – 2500	STM
Hard	Fails with firm sustained pressure	2500 - 4000	STH
No Shear	No shear failure observed		STN

2.7.3 Rutschblock Test

The Rutschblock (or glide-block) test is a slope test that was developed in Switzerland in the 1960s. This section is based on analysis of rutschblock tests in Switzerland (Föhn, 1987a; Schweizer, 2002) and Canadian (Jamieson and Johnston, 1993a and 1993b).

Equipment

Ski pole mounted saws or rutschblock cutting cords (eight meters of 4 to 7 mm cord with overhand knots tied every 20 or 30 cm) are great time savers for isolating the block in soft or medium hard snowpacks. However, it is often difficult to see the entire length of a cut made by these methods and extra care is needed to ensure the block has straight edges. Large rutschblock saws are useful to cut knife-hard crusts. The Rutschblock Test can be performed with either skis or a snowboard.

Figure 2.11 Stepping onto the block during a rutschblock test (photograph by Kelly Elder).

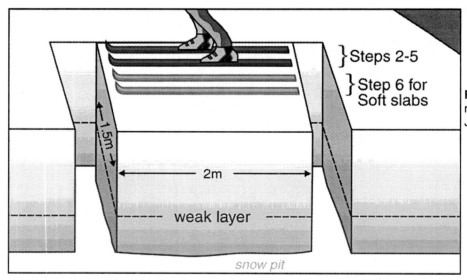

Figure 2.12 Schematic of the rutschblock test (after Jamieson and Johnston, 1993).

Snowpack Observations

Procedure
a) Select a safe site that has undisturbed snow and is geographically representative of the slopes of interest.
b) Observe a snow profile and identify weak layers and potential slabs.
c) Excavate a pit wall, perpendicular to the fall line, that is wider than the length of the tester's skis (2 m minimum)
d) Mark the width of the block (2 m) and the length of the side cuts (1.5 m) on the surface of the snow with a ski, ruler, etc. The block should be 2 m wide throughout if the sides of the block are to be dug with a shovel. However, if the side walls are to be cut with a ski, pole, or saw, the lower wall should be about 2.1 m across and the top of the side cuts should be about 1.9 m apart. This flaring of the block ensures it is free to slide without binding at the sides
e) Dig out the sides of the block, or make vertical cuts down the sides using the lines marked on the snow surface.
f) Cut the downhill face of the block smooth with a shovel.
g) Using a ski or snow saw make a vertical cut along the uphill side of the block so that the block is now isolated on four sides.
h) Rate any fractures that occur while isolating the block as RB1.
i) Conduct loading steps as described in Table 2.10, and record the results with the appropriate rutschblock score as well as the release type that occurred during the test (Table 2.11). A field book notation for recording rutschblock results is shown in Figure 2.13.
j) Rate any identified weak layers that did not fracture as no failure (RB7).

Record rutschblock results in a field book, along with pertinent site information using the method shown in Figure 2.13 or the data codes in Tables 2.8 and 2.11.

Table 2.10 Rutschblock Loading Steps and Scores

Field Score	Loading Step that produces a Clean Shear Fracture	Data Code
1	The block slides during digging or cutting.	RB1
2	The skier approaches the block from above and gently steps down onto the upper part of the block (within 35 cm of the upper wall).	RB2
3	Without lifting the heels, the skier drops once from straight leg to bent knee position (feet together), pushing downwards and compacting surface layers.	RB3
4	The skier jumps up and lands in the same compacted spot.	RB4
5	The skier jumps again onto the same compacted spot.	RB5
6	• For hard or deep slabs, remove skis and jump on the same spot. • For soft slabs or thin slabs where jumping without skis might penetrate through the slab, keep skis on, step down another 35 cm (almost to mid-block) and push once then jump three times.	RB6
7	None of the loading steps produced a smooth slope-parallel failure.	RB7

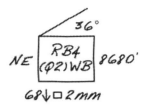

Figure 2.13 A field notebook method for recording a rutschblock score, release type, shear quality (center of box) along with the slope angle, elevation, crystal form and size, depth of weak layer, and aspect (clockwise from top). Arrows can be used to indicate whether the depth of the weak layer was measured from the snow surface or the ground (i.e. 68 cm below the snow surface).

Interpretation

No single measure is enough to determine the stability of a particular slope. The results of any stability test must be coupled with snowpack and weather histories, shear quality, snow structure, and other observations before the stability can be assessed.

Research in the Canadian Rocky Mountains has shown that:

Field score of 1, 2, or 3: The block fails before the first jump. The slope is unstable. It is likely that slopes with similar snow conditions can be released by a skier.

Field score of 4 or 5: The block fails on first or second jump. The stability of the slope is suspect. It is possible for a skier to release slab avalanches on slopes with similar snow conditions. Other observations or tests must be used to assess the slab stability.

Field score of 6 or 7: The block does not fail on the first or second jump. There is a low (but not negligible) risk of skiers triggering avalanches on slopes with similar snow conditions. Other field observations and tests, and safety measures remain appropriate.

Schweizer and Jamieson (2007) found that rutschblock scores combined with release type correlated well with observed avalanche occurrence. Johnson and Birkeland (2002) found that combining rutschblock scores with shear quality ratings reduced the number of false-stable results.

Limitations

The rutschblock is a good slope test but it is not a one-step stability evaluation. The test does not eliminate the need for snow profiles or careful field observations nor does it, in general, replace other slope tests such as slope cutting and explosive tests.

The rutschblock only tests layers deeper than ski penetration. For example, a weak layer 20 cm below the surface is not tested by skis that penetrate 20 cm or more. Higher and more variable rutschblock scores are sometimes observed near the top of a slope where the layering may differ from the middle and lower part of the slope (Jamieson and Johnston, 1993). Higher scores may contribute to an incorrect decision. The rutschblock may not effectively test weak layers deeper than about 1 m below ski penetration.

Table 2.11 Release Type Ratings for the Rutschblock Test

Term	Description	Data Code
Whole block	90 — 100% of the block	WB
Most of block	50 — 80% of the block	MB
Edge of block	10 — 40% of the block	EB

2.7.4 Compression Test

The compression test was first used by Parks Canada Wardens working in the Canadian Rockies in the 1970s. The following procedure was developed by the University of Calgary avalanche research project in the late 1990s. Similar tests have been developed elsewhere.

Objectives

The compression test identifies weak snowpack layers and is most effective at finding weak layers in the upper portion of the snowpack (~1 m). The tester taps a shovel blade placed on top of an isolated snow column causing weak layers within the column to fracture. These fractures can be seen on the smooth walls of the column. Compression test are typically performed on sloping terrain. Tests of distinct, collapsible weak layers can be performed on level study plots.

Equipment

A shovel is the only piece of equipment required for the Compression Test. However, a snow saw will make cutting the column of snow easier and more precise.

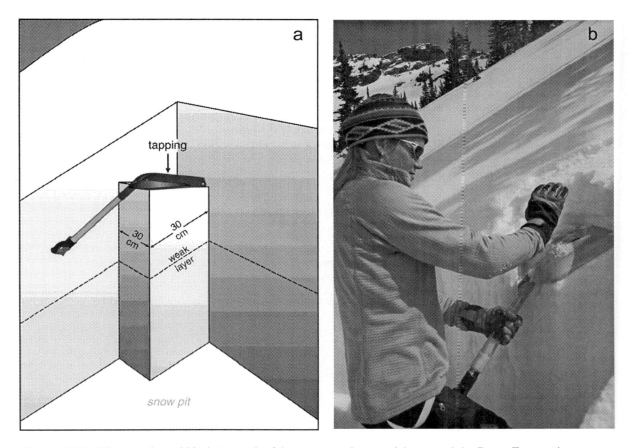

Figure 2.14 a) Schematic and b) photograph of the compression test (photograph by Bruce Tremper).

Procedure

a) Select a safe site that has undisturbed snow and is geographically representative of the slopes of interest.

b) Isolate a column of snow 30 cm wide and with a 30 cm upslope dimension that is deep enough to expose potential weak layers on the smooth walls of the column. Field tests have indicated that the size of the shovel blade to be used has minimal impact on test outcome (Jamieson, 1996). A depth of 100-120 cm is usually sufficient since the compression test rarely produces fractures in deeper weak layers. Also, taller columns tend to wobble during tapping, potentially producing misleading results for deep weak layers (Jamieson, 1996).

c) Rate any fractures that occur while isolating the column as very easy.

d) If the snow surface slopes, remove a wedge of snow to level the top of the column.

e) Place a shovel blade on top of the column. Tap 10 times with fingertips, moving hand from wrist and note the number of taps required to fracture the column (1 to 10).

f) If during tapping the upper part of the column slides off or no longer "evenly" supports further tapping on the column; remove the damaged part of the column, level the new top of the column and continue tapping.

g) Tap 10 times with the fingertips or knuckles moving forearm from the elbow, and note the total number of taps required to fracture the column (11 to 20). While moderate taps should be harder than easy taps, they should not be as hard as one can reasonably tap with the knuckles.

h) Finally, hit the shovel blade moving the arm from the shoulder 10 times with open hand or fist and note the total number of taps required to fracture the column (21 to 30). If the moderate taps were too hard, the operator will often try to hit the shovel with even more force for the hard taps – and may hurt his or her hand.

i) Rate any identified weak layers that did not fracture as no failure (CTN).

j) Record the depth of the snowpack that was tested. For example, if the top 110 cm of a 200 cm snowpack was tested (30 taps on a column, 110 cm tall) and the only result was a failure on the 15th tap, 25 cm below the surface, then record "CT15 @↓25 cm; Test depth 110 cm, or TD 110". This clearly indicates that no fracture occurred from 25-110 cm below the surface and that the snowpack between 110 cm and 200 cm was not tested with the Compression Test. Operations that always test the same depth of the snowpack, (e.g. top 120 cm) may omit the test depth.

Table 2.12 Loading Steps and Compression Test Scores

Term	Description	Data Code
Very Easy	Fractures during cutting	CTV
Easy	Fractures within 10 light taps using finger tips only	CT1 to CT10
Moderate	Fractures within 10 moderate taps from the elbow using finger tips	CT11 to CT20
Hard	Fractures within 10 firm taps from whole arm using palm or fist	CT21 to CT30
No Fracture	Does not fracture	CTN

Interpretation

The objectives of the compression test are to locate weak layers in the upper snowpack (approximately 1 m) and provide an indication of their triggering potential on nearby slopes with similar snowpack conditions. Deeper weak layers are generally less sensitive to the taps on the shovel resulting in higher ratings. Similarly, deeper weak layers are less sensitive to human triggering. Experience and research in the Rocky and Columbia Mountains of Western Canada indicates that human-triggered avalanches are more often associated with "easy" (1 to 9 taps) fractures than with "hard" (20 to 30 taps) fractures or with layers that do not fracture (Jamieson 1999). Sudden fractures (SC, SP, Q1) that show up on the column walls as straight lines identify the failure layers of nearby slab avalanches more often than non-planar or indistinct fractures (BRK, Q3) (van Herwijnen and Jamieson, 2003). The results of any stability test should be interpreted in conjunction with snowpack and weather histories, fracture type, and other snowpack and avalanche information

Limitations of the compression test include sampling a relatively small area of the snowpack and a variation in force applied by different observers. A greater understanding of these limitations can be gained by conducting more than one compression test in a snow profile and performing side by side tests with other observers at the beginning of the season.

2.7.5   Deep Tap Test

The Deep Tap Test was developed by the Applied Snow and Avalanche Research group at the University of Calgary. The test was developed to address very deep weak layers that are difficult to assess with other column and block tests.

Objective

The primary objective of the deep tap test is to determine the type of fracture that occurs in a weak layer that is too deep to fracture consistently in the Compression Test. In addition, it is possible to observe the tapping force required for fracture to occur.

Equipment

A shovel is the only piece of equipment required for the Deep Tap Test. However, a snow saw will make cutting the column of snow easier and more precise.

Table 2.13 Loading Steps and Deep Tap Test Scores

Term	Description	Data Code
Very Easy	Fractures during cutting	DTV
Easy	Fractures within 10 light taps using finger tips only	DT1 to DT10
Moderate	Fractures within 10 moderate taps from the elbow using finger tips	DT11 to DT20
Hard	Fractures within 10 firm taps from whole arm using palm or fist	DT21 to DT30
No Fracture	Does not fracture	DTN

Snow, Weather, and Avalanches

Procedure

a) Using a profile or other means, identify a weak snowpack layer, which is overlaid by 1F or harder snow and which is too deep to fracture consistently in the Compression Test.

b) Prepare a 30 cm x 30 cm column as for a Compression Test (note that the same column can be used after a Compression Test of the upper layers, provided the Compression Test did not disturb the target weak layer). To reduce the likelihood of fractures in weak layer below the target layer, such as depth hoar at the base of the snowpack, it may be advantageous not to cut the back wall more than a few centimeters below the target weak layer.

c) Remove all but 15 cm of snow above the weak layer, measured at the back of the sidewall. This distance should be constant, regardless of the slope angle.

d) Place the shovel blade (facing up or facing down) on top of the column. Tap 10 times with fingertips, moving hand from wrist and note the number of taps required to fracture the column (1 to 10).

e) Tap 10 times with the fingertips or knuckles moving your forearm from the elbow, and note the total number of taps required to fracture the column (11 to 20). While moderate taps should be harder than easy taps, they should not be as hard as one can reasonably tap with the knuckles.

f) Finally, hit the shovel blade moving arm from the shoulder 10 times with open hand or fist and note the total number of taps required to fracture the column (21 to 30). If the moderate taps were too hard, the operator will often try to hit the shovel with even more force for the hard taps – and may hurt his or her hand.

g) Record the results as described in Table 2.13. Observers may also include the total depth of the weak layer below the snow surface at the location of the test.

h) Use one of the methods in Section 2.6 to describe the type of fracture observed during the test. This information is important for deep, persistent weak layers.

Limitations

While very effective for testing deeper weak layers, the number of taps required to initiate a fracture in the Deep Tap Test has not been correlated with human-triggered avalanches or avalanches on adjacent slopes.

2.7.6 Stuffblock Test

The Stuffblock test was developed at the Gallatin National Forest Avalanche Center (southwest Montana) during the mid 1990's. The test has become a popular forecasting tool that can be conducted with minimal additional equipment.

Table 2.14 Loading Steps and Stuffblock Test Scores

Term	Description	Data Code
Very Easy	Fractures during column isolation	SBV
Easy	Fractures during static load	SB0
Easy (drop height of 10 or 20 cm)	Fractures during dynamic load	SB drop height number (SB10, SB20, etc.)
Moderate (drop height of 30 or 40 cm)		
Hard (drop height of 50 cm to 70 cm)		
No Fracture	Does not fracture	SBN

Snowpack Observations

Objective

The test identifies weak snowpack layers and is most effective at finding weak layers near the snow surface. A known mass is dropped from a known height to produce a dynamic load on a snow column. The fracture can be seen on the sides of the column. The stuffblock test is generally performed on sloping terrain steeper than about 25 degrees (Birkeland and Johnson, 1999).

Equipment

a) Snow shovel (a flat-bladed shovel works best)
b) Snow saw
c) Stuff sack with graduated cord (10 cm (~ 4 in) increments) attached to the bottom. The stuff sack diameter should be no larger than the width of the shovel blade.
d) Weighing scale capable of measuring 4.5 kg (~ 10 lb)

Procedure

a) Select a safe site that has undisturbed snow and is geographically representative of the slopes of interest.
b) Pack 4.5 kg (10 lb) of snow into a stuff sack.
c) Isolate a column of snow 30 cm wide and with a 30 cm upslope dimension that is deep enough to expose potential weak layers on the smooth walls of the column. The test column is generally no more than 100-120 cm (~ 50 in) in height. The Stuffblock Test can be used to test deeper weak layers. Taller columns tend to wobble during loading, potentially producing misleading results for deep weak layers.
d) Rate any fractures that occur while isolating the column as very easy (record as SBV).
e) Place the shovel blade on top of the column so that the blade is horizontal and the handle points upwards (Figure 2.15). Support the handle with one hand.
f) Gently place the filled stuff sack onto the shovel blade, and record any resulting fractures.
g) Raise the stuff sack 10 cm above the shovel blade and drop it onto the shovel.
h) Continue to drop the stuff sack onto the shovel blade incrementing the drop height by 10 cm each time (ie: 10 cm, 20 cm, 30 cm, etc.). After each drop examine the column for a fracture. If a fracture occurs, record the depth of the sliding plane and stuff sack drop height. Then remove the loose block of snow and continue the test on the sliding surface. The depth of snow removed at each fracture should be recorded. Test results from the shortened column will not accurately reflect the absolute strength of weak layers deeper than the initial fracture.
i) Any identified weak layers that did not fracture after a drop of 70 cm should be rated as SBN.
j) Test results should be recorded with the test identifier and the drop height that produced the fracture (example: If the column fractured with a static load, record as SB0. If the column fractured after a drop from 10 cm, record as SB10).
k) Record the depth of the snowpack that was tested. For example, if the top 110 cm of a 200 cm snowpack was tested and the result was a fracture 25 cm below the surface produced by a 20 cm drop, then record "SB20 @↓25 cm; Test depth 110 cm, or TD 110". This clearly indicates that no fracture occurred from 25-110 cm below the surface and that the snowpack between 110 cm and 200 cm was not tested with the stuffblock test. Operations that always test the same depth of the snowpack (e.g. top 120 cm) may omit the test depth.

Interpretation

The objectives of the stuffblock test are to locate weak layers in the upper snowpack (approximately 1 m) and provide an indication of the potential for human triggered avalanches on nearby slopes with similar snowpack conditions. Deeper weak layers are generally less sensitive to drops of the stuff sack, which results in higher test scores. Similarly, deeper weak layers are less sensitive to human triggering. Research conducted in the United States has shown that stuffblock test scores correlate to rutschblock

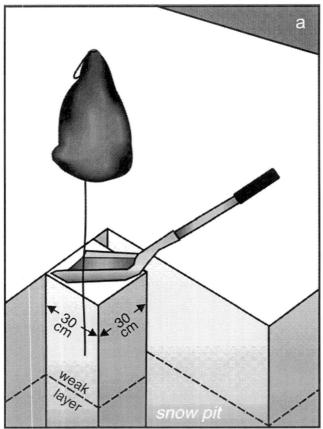

Figure 2.15 a) Schematic and b) photograph of the stuffblock test (photograph courtesy of the USDA Forest Service).

Snowpack Observations

test scores in a variety of snow climates (Birkeland and Johnson, 1999). The results of any stability test should be interpreted in conjunction with snowpack and weather histories, shear quality and other snowpack and avalanche information.

2.7.7   Extended Column Test

The Extended Column Test (ECT) was developed in Colorado and New Zealand in 2005 and 2006. The ECT has been tested in the continental and intermountain snow climates of the U.S. (Simenhois and Birkeland 2007; Hendrikx and Birkeland, 2008;Birkeland and Simenhois 2009), the Swiss Alps (Winkler and Schweizer 2009), the Spanish Pyrenees (Moner et al. 2008) and New Zealand's Southern Alps (Simenhois and Birkeland 2006, Hendrikx and Birkeland 2008).

Objective

The Extended Column Test (ECT) is a snowpack test that aims to test the fracture propagation propensity of slab/weak layer combinations in the upper portion of the snowpack (< 1m). The tester dynamically loads the snowpack by tapping on a shovel blade placed at one end of an isolated extended column in order to initiate a fracture (Figure 2.16). Once initiated, the key observation in the test is whether or not the fracture immediately propagates across the entire column.

Equipment

The equipment required for the ECT includes:

a) A snow shovel.

b) One or two collapsible probes or ski poles, 2 meter of 4-7 mm cord with knots every 20-30 cm or a snow saw with extension.

Procedure

a) Select a safe site that has undisturbed snow and is geographically representative of the slope of interest.

b) Isolate a column of snow 90 cm wide in the cross slope dimension and 30 cm deep in the upslope dimension that is deep enough to expose potential weak layers. Depth should not exceed 100 – 120 cm since the loading steps rarely affect deeper layers.

c) Rate any fractures that cross the entire column while isolating it as ECTPV.

d) If the snow surface slopes and the surface snow is hard, remove a wedge of snow to level the top of the column at one edge.

e) Place the shovel blade on one side of the column. Tap 10 times moving hand from the wrist and note the number of taps it takes to initiate a fracture and whether or not the fracture immediately propagates across the entire column on that or the next loading step (1 to 10).

f) Tap 10 times with the fingertips or knuckles moving forearm from the elbow and note the number of taps it takes to initiate a fracture and whether or not the fracture immediately propagates across the entire column on that or the next loading step (11 to 20).

g) Finally, hit the shovel blade moving arm from the shoulder 10 times with open hand or fist. Note the number of taps it takes to initiate a fracture and whether or not the fracture immediately propagates across the entire column on that or the next loading step (21 to 30).

h) If no fractures occurred within all loading steps, rate the test as ECTX.

i) If a fracture initiated on a weak layer on the ## tap but did not propagate across the entire column on the same or the next loading step, rate that layer as ECTN##.

j) If a fracture initiated and propagated across the entire column on the ## tap *or* it initiated on the ## tap and propagated on the ## + 1 tap, rate that layer as ECTP##.

Recording and Results
ECT recording describes if fractures initiated during the loading steps and whether or not those fractures immediately propagated across the entire column.

Interpretation
Test interpretation is straightforward. ECTPV and ECTP## results suggest unstable conditions, while ECTN## or ECTX are generally indicative of stable conditions. However, the objective of this test is to assess the propagation potential of the snowpack, therefore, ECTX should not necessarily be considered a sign of stability. In these cases other stability tests should be conducted to assess snowpack stability.

Strengths and Limitations
Two strengths of the ECT are its ease of interpretation (does the fracture propagate or not?) and the low false-stability ratio for the test, which is generally less than that for other typical tests. It is limited in that it is not a good tool to assess weaknesses in soft (F+ or less) upper layers of the snowpack or in mid-storm shear layers. In these cases the shovel edge tends to cut those soft layers. Further, the ECT is not a good tool to asses fracture propagation potential on a weak layer deeper than 100 – 120 cm because fracture initiation in these cases can be difficult or impossible (ECTX). In cases where a fracture is not initiated, other stability tests should also be conducted or a snowpit in different location should be considered.

Table 2.15 Extended Column Test Scores

Description	Data Code
Fracture propagates across the entire column during isolation	ECTPV
Fracture initiates and propagates across the entire column on the ## tap *or* the fracture initiates on the ## tap and propagates across the column on the ## + 1 tap	ECTP##
Fracture initiates on the ## tap, but does not propagate across the entire column on either ## or the ##+1 tap. It either fractures across only part of the column (observed commonly), or it initiates but takes more than one additional loading step to propagate across the entire column (observed relatively rarely).	ECTN##
No fracture occurs during the test	ECTX

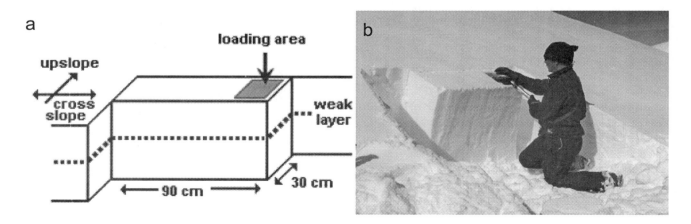

Figure 2.16 a) Schematic and b) photograph of the Extended Column Test (photograph courtesy of Ron Simenhois)

2.7.8 Propagation Saw Test

The Propagation Saw Test (PST) was simultaneously developed in Canada (Gauthier and Jamieson, 2007) and in Switzerland (Sigrist, 2006). The PST has been tested in Canada since 2005 – mostly in the Columbia Mountains, in the Swiss Alps and in Colorado's continental snowpack (Birkeland and Simenhois, 2008). The PST has been shown to indicate propagation propensity in persistent weak layers (PWL) buried 30 cm to over 100 cm and occasionally up to 250 cm deep.

Objective

The Propagation Saw Test is a snowpack test that aims to indicate the tendency (propensity) of a pre-identified slab and a PWL combination to propagate a fracture. The tester uses an isolated column and initiates a fracture by dragging a snow saw along the weak layer in the uphill direction.

Equipment

The equipment required for the PST includes:

A snow shovel.

A snow saw with a blade at least 30 cm long and approximately 2 mm thick.

For layers much deeper than the saw is long, the following are recommended

One or two collapsible probes.

Three to five meters of four to seven mm cord with knots every 20 – 30 cm.

Procedure

The PST procedure involves three main steps (after Gauthier and Jamieson, 2007): Identifying the weak layer of interest within the snowpack, isolating and preparing the test column, performing the test, and noting the results.

a) Select a safe site that has undisturbed snow and is geographically representative of the slope of interest.

b) Isolate a column 30 cm wide across the slope and 100 cm long upslope when the weak layer is less than 100 cm deep. (For layers deeper than the saw is long, two adjacent walls can be cut with a cord between probes.) When the weak layer is >100 cm deep the column length is equal to the weak layer depth in the upslope direction. The column should be isolated to a depth greater than the tested layer's depth.

c) To identify the weak layer clearly, mark the weak layer with a glove, a brush or a crystal card along the exposed column wall.

d) Drag the blunt edge of the saw upslope through the weak layer at a 10-20 cm/s speed until the fracture propagates (jumps) ahead of the saw, at which point the tester stops dragging the saw and marks the spot along the layer where propagation began.

e) After observations are complete, remove the column and check that the saw scored the weak layer in the wall behind the test column. If the saw deviated from the weak layer, the test should be repeated.

Results

Once the fracture propagates ahead of the saw, one of three results can be observed as noted in Table 2.16.

Interpretation

Fracture propagation is considered to be likely only if the fracture propagates to the end of the column, along the same layer and when the length of the saw cut is less then 50% of the column length when propagation begins (Gauthier and Jamieson, 2008). Otherwise, fracture propagation is considered unlikely (i.e. the propagating fracture failed to reach the end of the column or propagation begins when saw cut is greater than 50% of the column length).

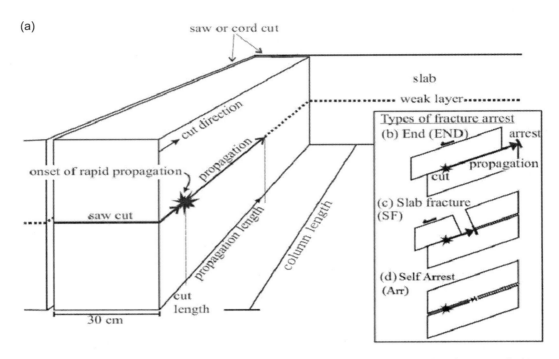

Figure 2.17 Schematic showing the PST column (a) and the observable results of propagation to end (b), slab fracture (c), and self arrest (d) (after Gauthier and Jamieson, 2007).

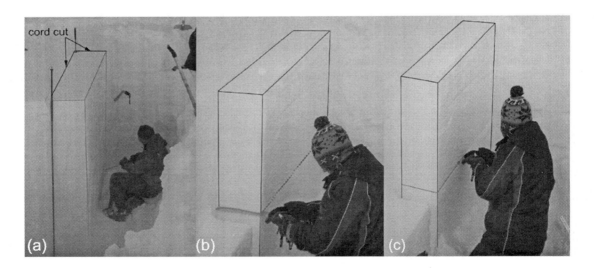

Figure 2.18 The PST process: (a) isolating the column with probes and cord; (b) identifying the weak layer and preparing to cut; (c) dragging the saw along the weak layer until the onset of propagation. Lightly brushing the weak layer with a glove or brush before cutting helps the operator follow the layer along the column (photo: ASARC).

Snowpack Observations

Table 2.16 Propagation Saw Test Description and Data Codes

Observed Result	Description	Data code
Propagation to end	The fracture propagates in the weak layer in front of the saw uninterrupted to end of column.	End
Slab fracture	The fracture propagates in the weak layer in front of the saw and stops where it meets a fracture through the overlying slab	SF
Self-arrest	The fracture propagates in front of the saw but self-arrests somewhere along the weak layer before reaching the end of the column.	Arr

Recording

The recording standard for the PST is as follows: '**PST x/y (Arr, SF or End) down z on yymmdd**' where x is the length of the saw cut when propagation starts, y is the length of the isolated column, z is the depth to the tested weak layer, and *yymmdd* is the weak layer identification typically dated by when the layer was buried. An example of a result that indicates high propagation propensity is 'PST 34/100 (End) down 56 cm on 080223'. It is recommended to comment on slope angle at the test site if it is not done on a 30-40°, as the cut distance (x) may depend on slope angle.

Strengths and Limitations

Because the PST is not dependent on surface loading, it is capable of assessing the propagation propensity of deeply buried weak layer and slab combination (deep instability). The PST is limited in that it has been shown to indicate a higher number of false-stable results than other common snowpack tests (around 30% for the PST versus approximately 10% for CTs, RBs and SBs), particularly for soft shallow slabs and when the weak layer is too hard to cut with the saw's blunt edge (Birkeland and Simenhois, 2008; Gauthier, D., Jamieson, J.B., 2008). Pre-selecting and identifying the layer of concern for testing can be challenging. Propagation to End occurs on flats as well as on incline slopes; however, as mentioned above, the cut distance (x) may depend on the slope angle.

2.8   Slope Cut Testing

Slope cutting can provide valuable information on snowpack stability. Safety must be the primary concern when attempting slope cuts, and inexperienced observers should not conduct this type of testing. Slope cut testing is typically applied to weak layers fairly near the snow surface, and soft snow slabs. Deeply buried weak layers and hard slab conditions often produce dangerous avalanches that break in less predictable locations and could prove dangerous, or fatal, to the tester.

There are many different approaches and "tricks of the trade" that can be applied to slope cutting. All of them are beyond the scope of this discussion. Slope cutting techniques should only be taught in the field or as "on the job training". More information on slope cuts can be found in McClung and Schaerer (1993) and Perla and Martinelli (1976).

Table 2.17 Slope Cut Testing Scores

Term	Description	Data Code
No release	No result	SCN
Whumpfing	Slope cut produces a collapse in the snowpack	SCW
Cracking	Slope cut produces shooting cracks	SCC
Avalanche Slab	Slope cut produces a slab avalanche	SCS
Avalanche Loose	Slope cut produces a loose snow or sluff avalanche	SCL

Figure 2.19 Slope cut producing a small slab avalanche (photograph by Bruce Tremper).

Procedure

- Choose a relatively small slope that is representative of the starting zones you wish to learn about.
- Place one or more people in zones of safety that allow them to observe the entire cut and avalanche path if possible.
- Begin from a zone of safety.
- Examine the starting zone and choose a line that crosses relatively high on the slope and ends in a zone of safety.
- Travel along the line chosen maintaining enough speed to cross the slope in one fast motion. The tester can bounce or jump during the cut to increase the load on the slope.
- Record the results of the test as described in the following section.

Recording Slope Cuts

Record the results of the test using the data codes listed in Table 2.17 along with the aspect and slope angle of the slope. When a ski cut produces a slab avalanche the Avalanche Size (Relative and/or Destructive) can be included in the data code. Additional information about the terrain and resulting avalanche can be recorded in comments as needed.

Example:

SCW35NE—Test produced a collapse (whumpf) on a 35° northeast facing slope
SCL40S—Test produced a sluff on a 40° south facing slope
SCN30N—Test produced no result on a 30° north facing slope
SCS45NWR3D2—Test produced a slab avalanche on a 45° slope that faces to the northwest. The avalanche was only medium in size, for the size of the path, but was large enough to injure or kill a person.

Snowpack Observations

2.9 Non-Standardized Snow Tests

All of the stability tests described in chapter two were developed from many years of work by many observers. Each test went through several iterations before a standard procedure was established. Field practitioners and researchers eventually wrote protocols and conducted research on these tests to provide information on their response and suitability.

In addition to the standardized tests, there are many other tests that do not have specific field protocols. In this section, some of the more common non-standardized snow tests and suggested methods for communicating their results are presented. Field workers who are not satisfied with the standardized tests are encouraged to seek additional methods for determining physical properties of the snowpack. As new methods evolve and we learn more about their response and limitations, those methods may become standard practice.

2.9.1 Communicating the Results of Non-Standardized Snow Tests

There is no standard method for communicating the results of non-standardized tests. A common method is to rate the amount of energy required to produce a fracture using the descriptors Easy, Moderate, or Hard (with easy being the smallest amount), and note the height of the resulting fracture. Suggestions for communicating specific tests are presented below.

2.9.2 Cantilever Beam Test

Most of the standardized snow tests examine a weak snow layer or interface between snow layers. This type of information is critical for determining the snow stability. However, the weak layer is only one component of a slab avalanche and knowing more about the mechanical properties of the slab is also useful.

Several investigators have used cantilever beam tests to examine mechanical properties of snow beams and snow slabs (Johnson and others, 2000; Mears, 1998; Sterbenz, 1998; Perla, 1969). Sterbenz (1998) describes a cantilever beam test developed for avalanche forecasting in the San Juan Mountains of Colorado and that test is presented below.

Procedure
a) Select a geographically representative site and dig a test profile.
b) Collect snowpack data as needed and conduct stability tests as desired.
c) Identify weak layer or interface and potential snow slab.
d) Above a smooth pit wall, mark a horizontal section of the slab 1 m (or 40") in length on the snow surface.
e) Mark 1 m (or 40") lengths perpendicular to the pit wall so a 1 m x 1 m square block is outlined on the snow surface.
f) At the identified weak layer, remove the supporting snow from below the slab to be tested (1 m x 1 m square block).
g) Using a snow saw, make a vertical cut 0.5 m (or 20") along one side of the block.
h) Using a snow saw, make a vertical cut 0.5 m (or 20") along the other side of the block.
i) Using a snow saw, extend the first cut an additional 0.5 m (or 20") so that one side of the 1 m x 1 m square block is isolated.
j) Using a snow saw, extend the second cut an additional 0.5 m (or 20") so that the other side of the 1 m x 1 m square block is isolated.
k) At this point the block should be suspended, with its only connection point along the uphill edge of the block. Place a shovel along the downhill side of the block and strike it with successive blows until the beam breaks.
l) Record with the data codes in Table 2.18.

57

Cantilever Beam Test References

Johnson, B.C., J.B. Jamieson, and C.D. Johnston. 2000: Field studies of the cantilever beam test. *The Avalanche Review,* **18,** 8-9.

Mears, A., 1998: Tensile strength and strength changes in new snow layers. *Proceedings of the International Snow Science Workshop,* Sunriver, Oregon, 574-576.

Perla, R.I., 1969: Strength tests on newly fallen snow. *Journal of Glaciology,* **8,** 427-440.

Sterbenz, C., 1998: The cantilever beam or "Bridgeblock" snow strength test. *Proceedings of the International Snow Science Workshop,* Sunriver, Oregon, p. 566-573.

Table 2.18 Cantilever Beam Test from Sterbenz (1998)

Loading Step	Block Breaks When
0	Removing snow from below the block.
1	0.5 m cut along one side.
2	0.5 m cut along the second side.
3	1 m cut along the first side.
4	1 m cut along the second side.
5	Loading the block that is isolated on three sides.

2.9.3   Loaded Column Test

The loaded column test (Figure 2.20) allows an observer to estimate how much additional mass a weak layer might support before it will fracture. Although this test can produce a finite mass that will produce fracture, the results of this test should be regarded only as a general indicator of the additional load that the snowpack can sustain. As stated previously, operational decisions should not be made on a single number or test.

Procedure

a) Select a geographically representative site and dig a test profile.
b) Collect snowpack data as needed and conduct stability tests as desired.
c) Identify weak layer or interface and potential snow slab
d) Using a snow saw isolate a column 30 cm wide and 30 cm in the upslope direction.
e) Excavate blocks of snow and stack them on the column until the column fractures.
f) Note the level of the fracture, shear quality, and amount of load that caused the test column to fail.
g) The mass of each block can be measured and a total load calculated.

a2.9.4 Burp-the-Baby

This test is generally used to identify shear layers missed by the shovel shear test. Buried thin weak layers (often surface hoar) gain strength over time and their presence may be obscured or missed by the shovel shear test.

Procedure

When an isolated column remains intact after it breaks on a deeply buried layer, pick it up and cradle it in your arms. Burp the reclining column across your knee or with a hand. Clear shear planes can often be located above the original shovel shear plane.

Figure 2.20 Two non-standardized snow tests: a) the shovel tilt test (photograph by Howie Garber) the loaded b) column test (photograph by Andy Gleason).

2.9.5 Hand Shear Tests

These tests can be used to quickly gain information about snow structure. They should not be used to replace stability tests, but can be used to estimate the spatial extent of a relatively shallow weak layer (Figure 2.22).

Procedure
a) With your hand or a ski pole make a hole in the snow deeper than the layer you wish to test.
b) Carve out an isolated column of snow.
c) Tap on the surface or pull on the column of snow in the down slope directions.
d) Record your results with the name of the test and rate the result as Easy, Moderate, or Hard (example: Hand Easy or Hand-E). Also include pertinent terrain parameters such as slope angle, aspect, and elevation.
e) Use other methods to investigate the weak layer or interface as needed.

2.9.6 Ski Pole Penetrometer

The ski pole can be used like a penetrometer to look for or estimate the spatial extent of distinct weak layers or significant changes in layer hardness (Figure 2.21). In harder snow, an avalanche probe can be used.

Procedure
a) Place the ski pole perpendicular to the snow surface and push it into the snow (Basket end down for soft snow, handle down for harder snow).
b) Feel for changes in resistance as the ski pole moves through the snowpack.
c) Feel for more subtle layers as the pole is removed from the snowpack by tilting it slightly to the side.
d) Record the depth, thickness and spatial extent of buried layers.
e) Use other methods to investigate the snowpack as needed.

Figure 2.21 The ski pole poke, aka ski pole penetrometer (photograph by Bruce Tremper).

2.9.7 Tilt Board Test

This description follows material published in McClung and Schaerer (1993). The Tilt Board Test is typically used to identify weaknesses in new snow or storm snow layers. The test is generally conducted at an established study plot. It can be used to identify weak layers that will be tested with a shear frame.

Equipment
- Thin metal plate 30 cm x 30 cm
- Tilt Board – a board painted white and mounted on a frame. The frame is mounted to a joint that allows it to rotate in the vertical plane. The Tilt Board can be locked in the horizontal position or tilted about 15 degrees. This allows the test block to fracture in shear without sliding off the lower portion of the block.

Procedure
a) Cut a block of snow that is deeper than the suspected weak layer or that contains all of the new or storm snow. McClung and Schaerer (1993) recommend using a block no deeper than 0.4 m.
b) Using a thin metal plate, lift the block on to the Tilt Board.
c) Tap the bottom of the board until the snow fractures.
d) Record your results with the name of the test and rate the result as Easy, Moderate, or Hard (example: Tilt Board Easy or Tilt Board-E).
e) Use other methods to investigate the weak layer or interface as needed.

2.9.8 Shovel Tilt Test

The shovel tilt test is the field worker's version of the Tilt Board Test but requires no additional equipment be taken into the field (Figure 2.20).

Procedure
a) Isolate a column of snow of similar dimensions to your shovel blade.
b) Insert the shovel blade horizontally into the side of the column below the layers you wish to test (limited to about 0.4 m from the surface).
c) Lift the shovel and snow sample into the air and hold the shovel handle and bottom of the snow column in one hand,
d) Tilt the shovel blade about 5 to 15 degrees steeper than the slope angle of the sample.
e) Tap the bottom of the shovel blade with increasing force until fracture is observed.
f) Record the force required to produce the fracture as Easy, Moderate, or Hard.
g) Shovel tilt may be increased and angle recorded if no fracture occurs at 15 degrees.
h) Use other methods to investigate the weak layer or interface as needed.

Figure 2.22 A hand shear test (photograph by Bruce Tremper).

2.10 Instrumented Methods
2.10.1 Ram Penetrometer

Objectives

The ram penetrometer is used to obtain a quantifiable measure of the relative hardness or resistance of the snow layers. It can be applied on its own as an index of snow strength, but it is not recommended as the sole tool for determining snow stability. When used in combination with a snow profile, a ram profile should be taken about 0.5 m from the pit wall after observation of the snow profile, but before any shovel shear tests are performed. It is a valuable tool for tracking changes in relative hardness over time at study plots and slopes, or for measuring many hardness profiles over an area without digging pits.

Note: The ram profile describes the hardness of layers in the snowpack. However, it often fails to identify thin weak layers in the snowpack. Surface hoar layers or other weak layers that are one centimeter or less are difficult to detect. Its sensitivity is dependent on the hammer weight, particularly when used in soft or very soft snow. The magnitude of this problem may be reduced by using a lightweight hammer (500 g or less), or by using a powder or "Alta" ram (Perla, 1969).

Refer to Chapter 6 of *The Avalanche Handbook* (McClung and Schaerer, 1993) for a complete discussion on ram profiles.

Equipment

The standard ram penetrometer, also called ramsonde, consists of:

a) 1 m lead section tube with 40 mm diameter cone and an apex angle of 60°.
b) Guide rod and anvil.
c) Hammer of mass 2 kg, 1 kg, 0.5 kg, 0.2 kg or 0.1 kg.
d) One or two (1.0 m each) extension tubes.

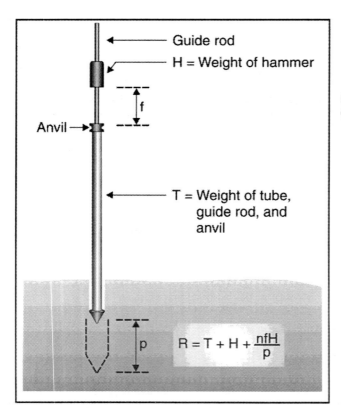

Figure 2.23 Schematic of the ram penetrometer (after Perla and Martinelli, 1976).

The powder ram, also called an Alta Ram (Perla, 1969), consists of:
  a) 0.50 m to 1.0 m lead section and guide rod and anvil weighing 100 g
  b) A hammer of mass 0.1 kg
  c) Lead section cone has the same dimensions as a standard ram
The mass of hammer chosen depends on the expected hardness of the snow and desired sensitivity.

Unit of Measure

A ram profile depicts the force required to penetrate the snow with a ram penetrometer. The mass of the tubes, the mass of the hammer, and the dynamic load of the falling hammer all contribute to the applied force. Ram profiles can display two different quantities: *ram number* (*RN*), which is a mass (kg), and *ram resistance* (*RR*), which is a force (N).

Weight is a gravity force that is calculated by multiplying mass with the acceleration due to gravity (9.81 m/s^2). Although not strictly correct, most practitioners multiply by 10 to simplify the calculations. Since the ram number is an index of hardness, there is little danger in rounding this value. Force, and consequently the ram resistance, are measured in newtons. A mass of 1 kg has a gravity force (weight) of 1 kg x acceleration which is approximately 10 N (1kg x 10m/s^2 =10N).

Procedure

Record the location, date, time, observers, slope angle, aspect, and ram type at the head of the data sheet. Also record any notes that will be pertinent to data analysis after leaving the field.

Work in pairs if possible. One person holds the ram penetrometer in a vertical (plumb) position with the guide rod attached. This person drops the hammer, counts the number of blows, and observes the depth of penetration. The other person records the information. The person holding the ram and dropping the hammer calls three numbers to the recorder: the drop number, drop height and penetration. For example, "5 from 20 is 143", means 5 drops from a drop height of 20 cm penetrated to 143 cm (Figure 2.22).

  a) Hold the first sectional tube with the guide rod attached directly above the snow surface with the point touching the snow. Let the instrument drop and penetrate the snow under its own weight without slowing it down with your hand. You will need to guide it in many cases so it does not fall over. Record its mass in column *T* + *H*. Read the penetration (cm) and record in column *p* (see Figure 2.22 for field data sheet example). Note that many people carry out this first step without attaching the guide rod first. However, since the tube weight *T* is 1.0 kg with the guide rod, it should be attached before the surface measurement is taken. Sometimes a greater sensitivity of the surface layer is desired. Dropping only the lead section without the guide rod will reduce the weight and may cause less of an initial plunge through the surface layers since the total mass will be lighter. If this method is used, then the weight of the lead section alone should be recorded for the *T* value, not the combined lead section and guide rod value of 1.0 kg.
  b) Carefully add the hammer, or guide rod and hammer if using the lead section only for the surface measurement. Record the mass of the tube + hammer under *T* + *H*. Read the new penetration and record under *p*. If the ram does not penetrate further, as is often the case in this step, record the previous *p* value again.
  c) Drop the hammer from a height between 1 cm and 5 cm; record the penetration. The low drop height (1-5 cm) is appropriate for near-surface layers. Larger drop heights (20-60 cm) and increased hammer weights may be desired as depth, and therefore, resistance increases. Continue dropping the hammer from the same height until the rate of penetration changes. Record fall height *f*, number of blows *n*, and penetration *p* up to the point. Some experience will allow the user to anticipate changes in the structure of the snow and record measurements before the rate of penetration changes. Continue with another series of blows; choose a fall height that produces a penetration of about 1 cm per blow. Do not change fall height or hammer weight within a series of measurements. Record the series then adjust fall

height or change hammer weight if desired before beginning another series. Resolution of the profile depends on the frequency of recorded measurements and the snowpack structure. Many recorded measurements in a homogeneous layer will provide no more resolution than fewer measurements since the calculated RN will be the same for both. However, resolution will be lost in varied layers if too many drops are made between recordings as the layer will receive a single RN over the entire range of p for that layer.

c) Add another section of tube when necessary and record the new $T + H$.

d) Repeat the measurements (b and c) until the ground surface is reached.

RAM DATA SHEET				
Location: Glory Bowl, Teton Pass, Wilson, WY				
Date: 19930312	Time: 0750 MST			
Observer: Newcomb/Elder				
Total depth: 239 cm	Equipment: Standard Ram			
Slope: 28°	Aspect E 80°			
Notes: 30 m south of GAZEX 1 Snowing 3cm/hr - wind SW 10m/s				
Tube and hammer wt $T + H$ (kg)	Number of falls n	Fall height f (cm)	Location of point L (cm)	Comments
1 + 0	0	0	23	tube & guide rod only, new snow deposited last 18 hr
1 + 0.5	0	0	25	add 0.5 kg hammer - no drop
	6	1	32	
1 + 1	0	0	32	change to 1 kg hammer
	4	5	37	
	11	10	49	
	7	20	52	crust
	5	10	64	
	15	10	87	
2 + 1	0	0	87	add 2nd tube section
	10	20	108	
	13	30	141	
	6	30	148	
3 + 1	0	0	148	add 3rd tube section
	25	30	181	
	22	30	209	
	1	30	215	
	3	10	239	

Figure 2.24 Sample field book page for Ram profiles.

Calculation

a) Calculate the increment of penetration p for each series of blows by subtracting the previous p value from the present p value (Figure 2.25).

b) Calculate ram number (RN) or ram resistance (RR) with the following equations:

$$RN = T + H + \frac{nfH}{p}$$

$$RR = RN \times 10$$

where:

RN = ram number (kg)
RR = ram resistance (N)
n = number of blows of the hammer
f = fall height of the hammer (cm)
p = increment of penetration for n blows (cm)
T = weight of tubes including guide rod (N) = 10 x mass (kg)
H = weight of hammer (N) = 10 x mass (kg)

c) Plot on graph paper the ram number or resistance vs. depth of snow (see Figure 2.26).

RAM CALCULATION SHEET								
Location: Glory Bowl, Teton Pass, Wilson, WY								
Date: 19930312	Time: 0750 MST							
Observers: Newcomb/Elder								
Total depth: 239 cm		Equipment: Standard Ram						
Slope: 28°		Aspect: E 80°						
Notes: 30 m south of GAZEX 1 Snowing 3cm/hr - wind SW 10m/s					$RN = T + H + (nfH)/p$ (kg) $RR = RN \times 10$ (N)			
Tube and hammer wt $T + H$ (kg)	Number of falls n	Fall height f (cm)	Location of point L (cm)	Penetration p (cm)	$(nfH)/p$ (kg)	RN (kg)	RR (N)	Height above ground (cm)
								239
1 + 0	0	0	23	23	0.0	1.0	10	216
1 + 0.5	0	0	25	2	0.0	1.5	15	214
	6	1	32	7	0.4	1.9	19	207
1 + 1	0	0	32	0				207
	4	5	37	5	4.0	6.0	60	202
	11	10	49	12	9.2	11.2	112	190
	7	20	52	3	46.7	48.7	487	187
	5	10	64	12	4.2	6.2	62	175
	15	10	87	23	6.5	8.5	85	152
2 + 1	0	0	87	0				152
	10	20	108	21	9.5	12.5	125	131
	13	30	141	33	11.8	14.8	148	98
	6	30	148	7	25.7	28.7	287	91
3 + 1	0	0	148	0				91
	25	30	181	33	22.7	26.7	267	58
	22	30	209	28	23.6	27.6	276	30
	1	30	215	6	5.0	9.0	90	24
	3	10	239	24	1.3	5.3	53	0

Figure 2.25 Sample work sheet page for calculating Ram profiles.

Snow, Weather, and Avalanches

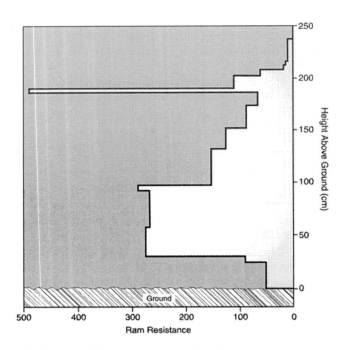

Figure 2.26 Graphical representation of a ram profile from data listed in Figures 2.22 and 2.23.

2.10.2 Shear Frame Test

The shear frame test is used to measure the shear strength of snow layers and interfaces between snow layers. The shear frame test requires experience, but provides useful information when done correctly and consistently. The test combined with a stability ratio is a useful tool for assessing the strength of snow layers. A list of useful references appears at the end of this section.

Equipment
The shear frame test requires the following equipment:
1) Putty knife
2) Metal cutting plate about 30 cm x 30 cm
3) Shear frame, usually 100 cm^2 or 250 cm^2
4) Force gauge, maximum capacity 10 to 250 N (1 to 25 kg).

If you are calculating the stability ratio, you will also need the following equipment:
5) Sampling tube
6) Weighing scale

Procedure
The shear frame test can be performed on storm snow layers and persistent weak layers. Typically 100 cm^2 frames are used for storm snow layers and 250 cm^2 are used for persistent weak layers. Observers generally perform 7 to 12 consecutive tests and average the results. Once a series of measurements is started it is important to not switch frame sizes.

1) Identify weak layer using tilt board or other method.
2) Remove the overlying snow to within 4 or 5 cm of the layer or interface being measured.
3) Carefully insert the shear frame into the snow so the bottom of the frame is 2 to 5 mm above the layer.
4) Pass a thin blade (putty knife) around the shear frame to remove snow that was in contact with the frame.
5) Attach an appropriate force gauge and pull so that fracture occurs within 1 second. This method ensures brittle fracture. It is essential that the operator loads the force gauge at a constant rate and is consistent between all measurements.

Snowpack Observations

Figure 2.27 Measuring the shear strength of a surface hoar layer with a 250 cm² shear frame and force gauge (photograph by Greg Johnson).

Shear Strength Calculation

Once you have obtained the average shear force for the weak layer or interface, calculate the shear strength from the formula:

$$T_{frame} = \frac{F_{average}}{A_{frame}}$$

where $F_{average}$ is the average shear force in newtons (N), A_{frame} is the area of the shear frame in m², and T_{frame} is the shear strength of the layer in pascals (Pa). This calculation produces a shear strength that is dependent on the shear frame size ($T_{frame} = T_{250}$ or T_{100}). For a value of shear strength that is independent of frame size use the following equations (Föhn, 1987b; Jamieson, 1995):

$$T_\infty = 0.65 \, T_{250}$$
$$T_\infty = 0.56 \, T_{100}$$

where T_∞ is the shear strength independent of shear frame size and T_{250} and T_{100} are the shear strengths measured with a 250 cm² and 100 cm² shear frame respectively.

Stability Ratios

The stability ratio is the shear strength of a layer divided by the overlying slab's weight per unit area. The stability ratio has a complex relationship with avalanche occurrence, but in general the lower the ratio the greater the likelihood of avalanches.

$$\text{Stability Ratio (SR)} = \frac{\text{shear strength}}{\text{weight per unit area}}$$

To determine the slab's weight per unit area, slide a small plate such as a putty knife or crystal card horizontally into the pit wall at a depth equal to the sampling tube length. Now slide the sampling tube vertically down through the surface until it strikes the plate. Excavate the sampling tube, taking care not to lose any snow out of the end of the tube. Transfer the contents of the sampling tube to a plastic bag for weighing. Divide the sample weight by the cross sectional area of the tube to calculate the slab weight per unit area.

Limitations

The shear frame works best for thin weak layers or storm snow interfaces. Thick weak layers (i.e. depth hoar) tend not to produce consistent fracture planes. The shear frame works poorly in situations where very hard layers (i.e. wind slabs and crusts) are directly above weak layers. The problem is inserting the shear frame into the hard layer without fracturing the weak layer below. In addition, there is little operational experience and literature on the use of shear frames with wet snow. The shear frame is also sensitive to user variability.

Shear Frame References

Föhn, P.M.B., 1987: The stability index and various triggering mechanisms. *Avalanche Formation, Movement, and Effects*, In: B. Salm and H. Gubler, (eds.), IAHS-AISH Publication No. 162, 195-211.

Jamieson, J.B., 1995: Avalanche prediction for persistent snow slabs, Ph.D. dissertation, University of Calgary, Calgary, Alberta. 53-58.

Jamieson, J.B., and C.D. Johnston, 2001: Evaluation of the shear frame test for weak snowpack layers. *Annals of Glaciology*, **32**, 59 - 66.

Perla, R.I., and T.M.K. Beck, 1983: Experience with shear frames. *Journal of Glaciology,* **29**, 485-491.

Roch, A., 1966: Les variations de la resistence de la neige. *Proceedings of the International Symposium on Scientific aspects of Snow and Ice Avalanches*. Gentbrugge, Belgium, IAHS Publication, 182-195.

Avalanche Observations

3.1 Introduction

Observations of past and present avalanche activity are of the utmost importance for any avalanche forecasting operation. These data should be recorded and organized in a manner that allows personnel to visualize temporal and spatial patterns in recent avalanche activity. Objectives for observing avalanches are presented in Section 3.2. A standard avalanche observation is presented in Section 3.4. The remainder of this chapter provides methods for observing a wide variety of avalanche related phenomena. Parameters are divided into avalanche path characteristics and avalanche event characteristics. Parameters in the standard avalanche observation are marked with a ✦ symbol. Individual operations can chose to observe and record parameters beyond those included in the standard observation. The parameters collected will depend on the type of operation and the snow climate of the forecast area.

3.2 Objectives

Observations and records of avalanche occurrences have the following applications:

- Information about avalanche occurrences and non-occurrences is used in association with other observations in evaluating snow stability.
- Observations identify areas where avalanches released earlier in the winter or storm/avalanche cycle. Snow stability may vary between these sites and nearby undisturbed slopes.
- Avalanche observation data are essential when protective works and facilities are planned, when the effectiveness of control measures is assessed, and when forecasting models are developed by correlating past weather and snow conditions with avalanche occurrences.
- Understanding the avalanche phenomenon through research.

All avalanches that are significant to an operation should be recorded. Noting the non-occurrence of avalanches is also important for snow stability evaluation and during hazard reduction missions.

3.3 Identification of Avalanche Paths

Avalanche paths should be identified by a key name, number, aspect, or a similar identifier which should be referred to on lists, maps, or photographs. For roads, railway lines and power lines it is convenient to refer to avalanche paths by the running mile or kilometer. Every effort should be made to retain historical names. Changing historical names creates confusing records and decreases the usefulness of past data records. Historical paths that have multiple starting zones can be reclassified with subcategories of the original name. Any reclassification should be clearly explained in the metadata (see Appendix C).

Avalanche paths with multiple starting zones are often divided into sub zones. Separate targets for explosive placement may be identified within each starting zone.

Figure 3.1 A slab avalanche (photograph by Jim Woodmencey).

3.4 Standard Avalanche Observation

This section outlines a standard avalanche observation for single avalanche events. Suggestions for summarizing multiple avalanche events are discussed in Section 3.7. Storm cycles and access to starting zones may make it difficult to observe every parameter for every avalanche that occurs within a forecast area. In this case the avalanche size characteristics should be estimated, and some of the snow specific parameters can be marked N/O for not observed.

The parameters have been separated into avalanche path characteristics and avalanche event characteristics. Operations that deal with a "fixed" number of paths documented in an avalanche atlas replace the path specific parameters with path name or number.

1) Date – record the date on which the avalanche occurred (YYYYMMDD).

2) Time – record the local time at which the avalanche occurred to the hour or minute if possible. Time codes of 2405 and 2417 can be used for avalanches that released at an unknown time during the AM and PM respectively. Time ranges or start and end times of control missions can also be used.

3) Observer – record the name or names of the personnel that made the observation.

4) Path Characteristics (Section 3.5)

    a. Observation Location – record the name or number of the path where the avalanche occurred, the latitude and longitude, or the nearest prominent topographic landmark (mountain, pass, drainage, etc.) or political landmark (town, road mile, etc.).

    b. Aspect – record the direction the slope faces where the avalanche occurred (i.e. N, NE, E, SE, S, SW, W, NW).

    c. Slope Angle in Starting Zone – record the **average** slope angle in the starting zone where the avalanche released. When possible, a number of locations in the starting zone should be measured so that a maximum, minimum, and average value can be reported.

    d. Elevation – record the elevation of the crown face in feet (meters).

5) Event Characteristics (Section 3.6)

    a. Type – record the avalanche type.

    b. Trigger – record the event that triggered the avalanche.

    c. Size – record the size of the avalanche.

    d. Snow Properties

        i. Bed Surface – record the location of the bed surface as: In new snow, New/old interface, in Old snow, or Ground. If the site was visited, record the hand hardness, grain type, and grain size.

        ii. Weak Layer – record the grain type and date of burial if known. If the site was visited record the hand hardness, grain type, and grain size.

        iii. Slab – record the hand hardness, grain type, and grain size.

    e. Dimensions

        i. Slab Thickness – record the **average** (and maximum) height of the crown face to the nearest 0.25 m (or whole foot).

        ii. Width – record the width (horizontal distance) of the avalanche to the nearest 10 m (or 25 feet).

        iii. Vertical Fall – record the vertical fall of the avalanche to the nearest 50 m (or 100 ft).

    f. Location of Start Zone – record the location of the crown face, as viewed from below, within the starting zone as top (T), middle (M), or bottom (B).

    g. Terminus – record the location of the debris within the avalanche path.

3.5 Avalanche Path Characteristics
3.5.1 Area and Path ✢

Enter the name of the operation or avalanche area where the avalanche path is located.

> *Note: It is not necessary to note the area in every entry of a field notebook if that book is not taken from area to area.*

Enter the identifier (name or number) of the avalanche path.

Some road operations may name their paths by the running mile or kilometer. In this case two decimal places may be used to identify paths within a whole mile or kilometer.

3.5.2 Aspect ✢

Use the eight points of compass to specify the avalanche's central aspect in the starting zone. Compass degrees or the sixteen major points (i.e. NNE, ENE, etc.) can be used to convey greater detail. A range in aspect can be specified for large or highly curved starting zones.

Table 3.1 Slope Aspect

Direction	N	NE	E	SE	S	SW	W	NW
Degrees	0	45	90	135	180	225	270	315

3.5.3 Slope Angle ✢

Record the average slope angle in the starting zone where the avalanche released. When possible, a number of locations in the starting zone should be measured so that a maximum, minimum and average value can be reported.

Figure 3.2 Measuring the slope angle of a slab avalanche (photograph by Bruce Tremper).

3.5.4 Elevation ✦

Record the elevation of the starting zone or crown face in feet (or meters) above sea level (ASL).

3.6 Avalanche Event Characteristics

3.6.1 Date ✦

Record year, month and day of the avalanche occurrence (avoid spaces, commas, etc.) i.e. December 15, 2001, is noted as 20011215 (YYYYMMDD).

3.6.2 Time ✦

Estimate the time of occurrence and record it by hour and minute in local standard time.

Record the time of occurrence on the 24-hour clock (avoid spaces, colons etc.) i.e. 5:10 p.m. is noted as 1710.

Use local standard time (i.e. Pacific, Mountain, etc.). Operations that overlap time zones should standardize to one time.

When the precise time of occurrence is unknown, use 2405 and 2417 for avalanches that released during the AM and PM respectively. Time ranges or start and end times of control missions can also be used.

3.6.3 Avalanche Type ✦

Record the type of avalanche as described in Table 3.2.

> *Note: A hard slab has an average density equal to or greater than 300 kg/m³. Informal distinctions can be made between hard and soft slab avalanches based on the form of the deposit and the hand hardness of the slab. Hard slab avalanches generally have a slab hardness of one finger or greater. Debris piles from hard slab avalanches are typically composed of angular blocks of snows.*

Table 3.2 Avalanche Type

Data Code	Type
L	Loose-snow avalanche
WL	Wet loose-snow avalanche
SS	Soft slab avalanche
HS	Hard slab avalanche
WS	Wet slab avalanche
I	Ice fall or avalanche
SF	Slush flow
C	Cornice fall (w/o additional avalanche)
R	Roof avalanche
U	Unknown

Avalanche Observations

Figure 3.3 Avalanche types: a) debris from a hard slab avalanche, b) wet slab, c) soft slab avalanche, d) point release avalanche or sluff (photographs by Karl Birkeland (a,b) and Bruce Tremper (c,d))

3.6.4 Trigger ✦

Indicate the mechanism that caused avalanche release with a primary code, secondary code when possible, and modifier when appropriate. The secondary codes have been separated into two categories with separate modifiers for each. Operations may devise other trigger sub-classes that apply to their specific conditions in consultation with the American Avalanche Association. Guidelines for reporting avalanche involvements are listed in Appendix H. Examples of coding structure are given in Section 3.6.12.

Table 3.3 Avalanche Trigger Codes - Primary

Data Code	Cause of Avalanche Release
N	Natural or Spontaneous
A	Artificial
U	Unknown

73

Snow, Weather, and Avalanches

Table 3.4 Avalanche Trigger Codes – Secondary-Natural and Explosive Releases

Data Code	Cause of Avalanche Release
Natural Triggers	
N	Natural trigger
NC	Cornice fall
NE	Earthquake
NI	Ice fall
NL	Avalanche triggered by loose snow avalanche
NS	Avalanche triggered by slab avalanche
NR	Rock fall
NO	Unclassified natural trigger (specify in comments)
Artificial Triggers: Explosive	
AA	Artillery
AE	An explosive thrown or placed on or under the snow surface by hand
AL	Avalauncher
AB	An explosive detonated above the snow surface (air blast)
AC	Cornice fall triggered by human or explosive action
AX	Gas exploder
AH	Explosives placed via helicopter
AP	Pre-placed, remotely detonated explosive charge
Artificial Triggers: Miscellaneous	
AW	Wildlife
AU	Unknown artificial trigger
AO	Unclassified artificial trigger (specify in comments)

Table 3.5 Avalanche Trigger Codes – Modifiers for Natural and Explosive Caused Releases

Data Code	Cause of Avalanche Release
r	A remote avalanche released by the indicated trigger
y	An avalanche released in sympathy with another avalanche

Note: For remote and sympathetic avalanches the distance between the trigger and the avalanche should be recorded in the comments.

Avalanche Observations

Table 3.6 Avalanche Trigger Codes – Secondary-Human Triggered Avalanches

Data Code	Cause of Avalanche Release
Artificial Triggers: Vehicle	
AM	Snowmobile
AK	Snowcat
AV	Vehicle (specify vehicle type in comments)
Artificial Triggers: Human	
AS	Skier
AR	Snowboarder
AI	Snowshoer
AF	Foot penetration
AC	Cornice fall produced by human or explosive action
Artificial Triggers: Miscellaneous	
AU	Unknown artificial trigger
AO	Unclassified artificial trigger (specify in comments)

Table 3.7 Avalanche Trigger Codes – Modifiers for Human Triggered Avalanches

Data Code	Cause of Avalanche Release
c	A controlled or intentional release by the indicated trigger (i.e. slope cut, intentional cornice drop, etc.).
u	An unintentional release.
r	A remote avalanche released by the indicated trigger
y	An avalanche released in sympathy with another avalanche

Note: For remote and sympathetic avalanches the distance between the trigger and the avalanche should be recorded in the comments.

Avalanches that start when a helicopter or other aircraft flies overhead should be considered natural if the aircraft is a significant distance above the ground.

Avalanches triggered by helicopters when in "ground effect" should be considered artificially triggered. Ground effect can be observed when significant rotor wash (blowing snow) is noticed on the snow surface below the helicopter. Use your best judgment.

3.6.5 Size ✦

The two commonly used avalanche size classification schemes are: Relative to Path and Destructive Force. Both systems use a scale that varies from 1 to 5. These guidelines recommend observing and recording avalanche size in both systems. Using both systems will maintain long-term data sets and provide the most useful information to active forecasting programs. However, forecasting program managers should decide whether to use one or both schemes. Each system provides different and useful information, but the numerical categories of each scale are often not comparable.

3.6.5.1 Size – Destructive Force

Estimate the destructive potential of the avalanche from the mass of deposited snow, and assign a size number. Imagine that the objects on the following list (people, cars, trees) were located in the track or at the beginning of the runout zone and estimate the harm the avalanche would have caused.

Table 3.8 Avalanche Size – Destructive Force (after CAA, 2000; Perla, 1980)

Data Code	Avalanche Destructive Potential	Typical Mass	Typical Path Length
D1	Relatively harmless to people	<10 t	10 m
D2	Could bury, injure, or kill a person.	10^2 t	100 m
D3	Could bury and destroy a car, damage a truck, destroy a wood frame house, or break a few trees.	10^3 t	1,000 m
D4	Could destroy a railway car, large truck, several buildings, or a substantial amount of forest.	10^4 t	2,000 m
D5	Could gouge the landscape. Largest snow avalanche known.	10^5 t	3,000 m

Note: The use of half-sizes may be used to signify an avalanche that is on the high end of a single class.

The destructive potential of avalanches is a function of their mass, speed and density as well as the length and cross-section of the avalanche path.

Typical impact pressures for each size number are given in McClung and Schaerer (1981).

The number "0" may be used to indicate no release of an avalanche following the application of mitigation measures.

Figure 3.4 Slab avalanche triggered by a loose-snow avalanche (photograph by Andy Gleason).

Avalanche Observations

3.6.5.2 Size – Relative to Path

The size—relative to path classification is a general measure and takes into account many factors, including the horizontal extent and vertical depth of the fracture, the volume and mass of the debris, and the runout distance of the avalanche. The observer estimates the size of the avalanche relative to the terrain feature or avalanche path where it occurred. A "small" avalanche is one that is relatively small compared to what that particular avalanche path could produce, while a "large" avalanche is, or is close to, the largest avalanche that the particular avalanche path could produce.

Table 3.9 Avalanche Size – Relative to Path

Data Code	Avalanche Size
R1	Very small, relative to the path.
R2	Small, relative to the path
R3	Medium, relative to the path
R4	Large, relative to the path
R5	Major or maximum, relative to the path

Note: Half-sizes should not be used for the size-relative to path scale.

The number "0" may be used to indicate no release of an avalanche following the application of mitigation measures.

The size classification pertains to both the horizontal extent and the vertical depth of the fracture, as well as the volume and runout distance of the avalanche.

3.6.6   Snow Properties
3.6.6.1   Bed Surface ✦
Level of Bed Surface

Record the level of the bed surface (the upper surface of the layer over which a slab slid) in the snowpack. If the avalanche involved more than one bed surface, all applicable codes should be included.

Table 3.10 Avalanche Bed Surface

Data Code	Bed Surface
S	The avalanche released within a layer of recent storm snow.
I	The avalanche released at the new snow/old snow interface.
O	The avalanche released within the old snow.
G	The avalanche released at the ground, glacial ice or firn.
U	Unknown

Note: Storm snow is defined here as all snow deposited during a recent storm.

Form and Age of Fracture Plane

Record the predominant grain form observed in the layer below the fracture plane using the *International Classification for Seasonal Snow on the Ground* (refer to Appendix F). Where possible identify the failure plane by its probable date of burial. Use the comments section to note the occurrence of a fracture that steps down to other layers.

3.6.6.2   Weak Layer ✦

Record the grain type using the *International Classification for Seasonal Snow on the Ground* (see Appendix F), grain size (mm), and hand hardness of the weak layer.

3.6.6.3   Slab ✦

Record the grain type using the *International Classification for Seasonal Snow on the Ground* (see Appendix F), grain size (mm), and hand hardness of the slab directly above the weak layer.

3.6.6.4   Liquid Water Content in Starting Zone and Deposit

Determine the liquid water content of the avalanche snow in the starting zone and deposit at the time of failure and deposition. The liquid water content can be different in the starting zone and deposit. Although these observations use the same data code, they can be recorded as two separate items to include more information.

Table 3.11 Liquid Water Content of Snow in Avalanche Starting Zone

Data Code	Liquid Water Content
D	Dry snow
M	Moist snow
W	Wet snow
U	Unknown

Note: See Table 2.4 for water content definitions.

3.6.7   Avalanche Dimensions

3.6.7.1   Slab Thickness ✦

If practical, estimate or measure the average and maximum thickness of the slab normal to the slope to the nearest 25 centimeters (or whole foot), the average thickness of the slab at the fracture line. Add "M" when thickness is actually measured. If only one value is reported it should be the **average** dimension.

3.6.7.2   Slab Width ✦

In a slab avalanche, record the width (horizontal distance) in meters (feet) of the slab between the flanks near the fracture line. Add "M" when width is actually measured.

3.6.7.3   Vertical Fall ✦

Using an altimeter or contour map, calculate the elevation difference in feet (meters) between the fracture line and debris.

Avalanche Observations

3.6.7.4 Length of Path Run

Some operations may wish to record the estimated distance an avalanche ran along a slope. Up to a distance of 300 m (~ 1000 ft) estimate the distance traveled to nearest 25 m (~ 100 ft). Beyond a distance of 300 m estimate the distance run to nearest 100 m (~ 300 ft).

Note: All dimensions are assumed to be estimates unless the values are followed with the letter M (measured).

Dimensions are assumed to be in meters. Measurements or estimates in feet should be indicated with a ' after the number (i.e. 3').

3.6.8 Location of Avalanche Start ✦
Position in Starting Zone

Describe the location of the avalanche fracture with one of the following code letters, physical features or elevation *and*, when applicable, add the data code for the starting sub-zone or the target.

Note: For this code gunner's left and right should be used. Gunner's perspective is looking up at the starting zone (opposite of skier's perspective).

Figure 3.5 An avalanche remotely triggered by a skier (SS-ASr-R2/D2-O) in the Wasatch Mountains, Utah (photograph by Bruce Tremper).

Snow, Weather, and Avalanches

3.6.9 Terminus ✦

Describe the location of the tip of the avalanche deposit with a code letter.

Table 3.12 Location of Avalanche Start

Data Code	Vertical Location within Starting Zone from Gunner's Perspective
T (L, R, C)	At the top of the starting zone (left, right, or center)
M (L, R, C)	In the middle of the starting zone(left, right, or center)
B (L, R, C)	At the bottom of the starting zone (left, right, or center)
U	Unknown

Note: The codes TP, MP and BP are applicable for short paths where the starting zone, track and runout zone cannot be easily separated.

Table 3.13 Terminus of Avalanche Debris

Data Code	Terminus for long paths
SZ	The avalanche stopped in the starting zone.
TK	The avalanche stopped in the track
TR	The avalanche stopped at the top part of the runout zone
MR	The avalanche stopped in the middle part of the runout zone
BR	The avalanche stopped in the bottom part of the runout zone
U	Unknown

Data Code	Terminus for short paths
TP	The avalanche stopped near the top of the path
MP	The avalanche stopped near the middle part of the path
BP	The avalanche stopped near the bottom part of the path

Operations that have large avalanche paths with well-defined features may apply additional codes (See Table 3.14).

Table 3.14 Detailed Terminus Codes

Data Code	Terminus
1F	Stopped on top ¼ of the fan
2F	Stopped halfway down the fan
3F	Stopped ¾ of way down the fan

80

Avalanche Observations

3.6.10   Total Deposit Dimensions
Record the average width and length of the deposited avalanche snow in meters (feet).

Record the average deposit depth in meters and tenths of a meter. Add an "M" after each value if measured by tape or probe.

3.6.11   Avalanche Runout
The angle between the horizontal and a line drawn from the highest portion of the crown face and the toe of the debris can be used as a relative measure of avalanche runout. This angle, known as the *alpha angle* (α), has been used by landslide investigators since the late 1800's and has been applied to avalanche studies to describe extreme (~100 year) events. Although in avalanche research α has generally been reserved for very large events, guide services, engineers, scientists, and forecasters may find the subcategories defined in Table 3.15 useful.

Table 3.15 Alpha Angle Subcategories

Data Code	Description
α_i	The measured alpha angle for any individual avalanche.
α_e	The alpha angle of an extreme event. The smallest alpha angle (furthest avalanche runout) observed in a specific avalanche path, determined by historical records, tree ring analysis, or direct observation.
α_{number}	A calculated value of the smallest alpha angle (furthest avalanche runout) in a specific avalanche path during a defined time period. Where the designated time period (return period) in years is listed in the subscript (α_{10}, α_{50}, α_{100}).

Statistical studies suggest that alpha angles in a specific mountain range can cluster around a characteristic value. This value may be governed by terrain and snowpack conditions characteristic of the range (McClung and Schaerer, 1993; Mears, 1992; McClung and others, 1989; Lied and Bakkehøi, 1980).

3.6.12   Coding Avalanche Observations
Avalanche observations can be recorded in tabular format with a separate column for each data code. Common data codes can also be recorded in one string.

Example:
HS-AA-R2-D2: a hard slab avalanche triggered artificially by artillery
SS-AE-R4-D3: a soft slab avalanche triggered artificially by a hand charge
L-N-R1-D1: a small loose snow avalanche triggered by a natural event
HS-ASr-R3-D3-O: a hard slab avalanche triggered remotely by a skier and broke into old snow layers (see Section 3.6.4)
HS-ACu-R4-D3: a hard slab avalanche triggered by an unintentional artificial cornice fall
HS-ACc-R2-D3: a hard slab avalanche triggered by an intentional artificial cornice fall
HS-AC-R2-D3: a hard slab avalanche triggered by a cornice drop produced by explosives
WS-NS-R4-D3: a wet slab triggered by a natural slab avalanche.
AC-0: An intentionally triggered cornice that did not produce an avalanche.

3.6.13   Comments
Enter information about damage and accidents caused by the avalanche and any other significant information. Note when the avalanche was triggered artificially. Use as much space as required.

Snow, Weather, and Avalanches

Table 3.15 Multiple Avalanche Events – Recording Example

Parameter	Criteria	Examples
Date or date range	Record beginning of cycle and end of cycle when possible.	20010212 or 20010212 – 20010214
Time range	Digits	0000 – 1000
Area (location)	Text (80 characters max.)	Mt. Timpanogos
Size	Attempt to limit the size range to 2 classes. Significant or very large avalanches should be recorded as individual events.	D1.5 – D2.0 R2-R3
Trigger	Data code (do not mix natural and artificial triggers in this report)	AE, U
Type	Data code (group slab and loose avalanches separately)	HS, SS, U or WL, U
Aspect (of starting zone)	A single, range, or a combination of compass directions.	All, W, SW – NW
Elevation (at fracture)	Group events by elevation range. Use separate reports for significant elevation ranges as applicable to forecast area.	5,000 – 6,500 and 8,000 –10,000 ft
Slope Angle (at fracture)	Record range in average starting zone angle and max and min	32–42, 30, 45
Level of bed surface	Key letter (do not mix storm snow, old snow, and ground)	S, O, G, or U
Hardness of bed surface	Hand hardness scale	1F
Weak layer grain form	Grain form abbreviation (Fierz et al., 2009)	SH
Hardness of weak layer	Hand hardness scale	4F
Age of failure plane	Probable date of burial	20011204
Slab width	Range (in meters)	60 – 110 m
Slab thickness	Range (in centimeters)	10 – 30 cm
Hardness of slab	Hand hardness scale	P
Vertical Fall	Range (in meters)	500 – 1500 m
Comments	Max. of 5 lines by 80 characters per line	

3.7   Multiple Avalanche Events

An operation may wish to group large numbers of similar avalanche events (avalanche cycle) into one record or report, especially if that information is to be sent to a central information exchange. Grouping is achieved by allowing certain fields to hold a range of values (i.e. by specifying lower and upper bounds, separated by a dash). The report should be repeated for different types of activity (i.e. natural versus artificially released avalanches).

Note: Significant avalanches (larger than size D3 or R3), and events involving incident, damage or injury should be described individually.

3.8 Additional Observations

Additional observations may be selected as applicable from those listed in this section. Certain additional observations are valuable in areas where avalanches are either controlled or affect traffic and/or communication lines.

3.8.1 Avalanche Hazard Mitigation Missions

3.8.1.1 Number of Explosive Charges / Number of Detonations

Record the number of projectiles or explosive charges applied to a target.

Record the number of confirmed detonations.

Note: The difference in the two values gives a dud count.

3.8.1.2 Size of Explosive Charge

Note the mass (kg) of the explosive charge used at each shot location.

3.8.2 Road and Railway Operations

3.8.2.1 Deposit on Road or Railway

Record in meters (feet) the length of road, railway line, ski run, power line, or other facility buried in avalanche snow.

Record average depth at center line and maximum depth of avalanche snow on the road, etc., in meters and tenths of a meter (feet/inches). Add "M" when length and depth are measured.

3.8.2.2 Distance to Toe of Deposited Mass

Measure or estimate the distance between the uphill edge of the road, or other development, and the farthest point reached by the mass of avalanche. Negative values are used when the deposited mass failed to reach the road or facility.

Note: Some operations may also wish to document the occurrence of snow dust on the road. Dust results from the fallout of an avalanche's powder cloud. Its main impact is on driver visibility.

3.8.2.3 Road / Line Status

Transportation operations should record the status (open or closed) and danger rating (Appendix G) in effect for any roads or railway lines at the time when the avalanche occurred. During closures due to control missions or avalanche activity, the start and end time of the closure should be recorded.

Figure 3.6 An avalanche triggered by glide of the snowpack (photograph by Bruce Tremper).

Snow, Weather, and Avalanches

Glossary

Accuracy—The difference between the measured value and the actual or true value. A property of a measurement method and instruments used. Also see **precision**.

Alpha Angle—The angle between the horizontal and a line drawn from the highest point of the **crown face** to the toe of the debris. Alpha can be measured for an individual avalanche (a_i). Extreme values of alpha (a_e) can be determined from historical records, tree ring data, or direct observation. Minimum values of alpha (longest runout length) can also be calculated for a specific return period (a_{10}, a_{50}, a_{100}). Also termed the angle of reach.

Anemometer—An instrument that measures the pressure exerted by, or the speed of wind.

Aspect—The exposure of the terrain as indicated by compass direction of the **fall line** (relative to true north). A slope that faces north has a north aspect.

Atmospheric Pressure—The pressure due to the weight of air on the surface of the earth or at a given level in the atmosphere. Also called **barometric pressure**.

Avalanche, Snow—A mass of snow sliding, tumbling, or flowing down an inclined surface that may contain rocks, soil, vegetation, or ice.

Avalanche Danger Scale—A categorical estimation of the avalanche danger. In the U.S., a five level scale is used for backcountry recreational users. See Appendix G.

Avalanche Path—A terrain feature where an avalanche occurs. An avalanche path is composed of a **starting zone**, **track**, and **runout zone**.

Avalauncher—A compressed gas delivery system for explosives. Designed for avalanche hazard mitigation.

Barometer—An instrument that measures **atmospheric pressure**. Barometers typically express this measure in millibars (mb) or inches of mercury (inHg).

Barometric Pressure—The pressure exerted by a column of air on the surface of the earth or at a given level in the atmosphere. Also called **atmospheric pressure**.

Bed Surface—The surface over which fracture and subsequent avalanche release occurs. The bed surface is often different than the **running surface** over which the avalanche flows through the track. A bed surface can be either the ground or a snow/ice surface.

Calibrate—To ascertain the error in the output of a measurement method by checking it against an accepted standard.

Caught—A category of the avalanche toll for an accident. A person is *caught* if they are touched and adversely affected by the avalanche. People performing slope cuts are generally not considered *caught* in the resulting avalanche unless they are carried downhill.

Collapse—When fracture of a lower layer causes an upper layer to fall, producing a displacement at the snow surface. The displacement may not always be detectable with the human eye. A collapse in the snowpack often produces a whumpfing sound.

Completely Buried—A category of the avalanche toll for an accident. A person is *completely buried* if they are completely beneath the snow surface when the avalanche stops. Clothing or attached equipment is not visible on the surface.

Concave Slope—A terrain feature that is rounded inward like the inside of a bowl (i.e. goes from more steep to less steep).

Snow, Weather, and Avalanches

Condensation—The process of a gas being converted to a liquid due to changes in **temperature** and/or **pressure**. Also see definition of **evaporation**.

Convex Slope—A terrain feature that is curved or rounded like the exterior of a sphere or circle (i.e. goes from less steep to more steep).

Cornice—A mass of snow that is deposited by the wind, often overhanging, and usually near a sharp terrain break such as a ridge.

Creep—The time-dependent permanent deformation (**strain**) that occurs under stress. In the snow cover this includes **deformation** due to **settlement** and internal shear.

Crown—The snow that remains on the slope above the **crown face** of an avalanche.

Crown Face—The top fracture surface of a slab avalanche. Usually smooth, clean cut, and angled 90 degrees to the **bed surface**. Also see **fracture line**.

Crystal—A physically homogenous solid in which the internal elements are arranged in a repetitive three-dimensional pattern. Within an ice lattice the internal elements are individual water molecules held together by hydrogen bonds. Usually synonymous with **grain** in snow applications (see definition for **grain)**, although the term grain can be used to describe multi-crystal formation.

Danger, Avalanche—The potential for an avalanche(s) to cause damage to something of value. It is a combination of the likelihood of triggering and the destructive size of the avalanche(s). It implies the potential to affect people, facilities or things of value, but does not incorporate vulnerability or exposure to avalanches. Avalanche danger and hazard are synonymous and are commonly expressed using relative terms such as high, moderate and low.

Debris, Avalanche—The mass of snow and other material that accumulate as a result of an avalanche.

Deformation, Solid—A change in size or shape of a solid body.

Density—A mass of substance per unit volume. The International System of Units (SI) uses kg/m^3 for density.

Deposition, Vapor—The process of a gas being converted directly to a solid due to changes in **temperature** and/or **pressure**. Also see definition for **sublimation**.

Deposition, Wind—The accumulation of snow that has been transported by wind.

Dew Point—The **temperature** at which water vapor begins to condense and deposit as a liquid while the **pressure** is held constant.

Equilibrium Vapor Pressure—The **partial pressure** at which **evaporation** and **condensation** are occurring at the same rate. Also see **saturation vapor pressure**.

Error—The difference between the output of a measurement method and the output of a measurement standard.

Evaporation—Strictly defined as the conversion of mass between liquid and gas phases due to changes in **temperature** and/or **pressure**. Commonly used to describe mass conversion from liquid to gas, with **condensation** describing a phase change in the opposite direction.

Exposure— An element or resource (person, vehicle, structure, etc…) that is subject to the impact of a specific natural hazard.

Glossary

Failure—A state of **stress** or **deformation** that meets a specific criterion. Many criteria for failure exist, but the most commonly used criteria for snow are: 1) the point at which shear **stress** in a weak layer equals the shear **strength**, 2) the point at which shear **deformation** increases while the **strength** of the weak layer decreases, 3) sudden excessive plastic **deformation**, 4) during a stability test, the loading step at which the test column **fractures**. Failure is a precursor to **fracture**, but fracture (and slab release) may or may not occur after failure. To avoid confusion, the criterion should always be specified when discussing failure.

Fall line—The natural downhill course between two points on a slope.

Flank—The snow to the sides of a slab avalanche, which remains after the release.

Force—An agent that causes acceleration or deformation of a particular mass. Often expressed by Newton's Second Law, $F = m \times a$, where the force acting on a given object is the product of its mass and its acceleration.

Fracture—The separation or fragmentation of a solid body into two or more parts under the action of **stress**. A discussion of fracture often encompasses two physical processes: crack initiation and crack propagation. Snow fracture can occur at different scales, from the rupture of ice bonds to the fracturing of a weak layer. Fracturing is a prerequisite for slab avalanche release, which occurs when the initial shear fracture, at the weak layer or interface at the **bed surface**, propagates to the **crown face**, **flank**s and **stauchwall**.

Fracture Line—The remaining boundary of a slab after an avalanche has occurred. Also see definitions for **crown face**, **flank** and **stauchwall**.

Fracture Mechanics - A branch of materials physics that is concerned with the initiation and propagation of fractures. The field generally utilizes three variables: applied stress, flaw size, and fracture toughness (a material property), to characterize crack energetics or crack stresses.

Full Profile—A complete snow profile observation where **grain** size, **grain** type, interval **temperature**, layer **density** and layer hardness are measured and recorded in addition to **stability** information.

Funicular, Wet Snow Regime—When discontinuous air spaces and continuous volumes of water exist in a snow cover. In a funicular snow cover only water-ice and air-liquid connections exist. It is generally assumed that snow with a liquid water content (by volume) of 8 - 15 % is in the funicular regime. Also see the definition for the **pendular** regime.

Glide—Downhill slip of the entire snowpack along the ground or firm interface.

Grain—The smallest distinguishable ice component in a disaggregated snow cover. Usually synonymous with **crystal** in snow applications. The term grain can be used to describe polycrystal formations when the crystal boundaries are not easily distinguishable with a field microscope.

Hang Fire—Snow adjacent to an existing **fracture line** that remains after avalanche release. Hang fire typically has a similar **aspect** and **incline** to the initial avalanche.

Hard Slab—A snow **slab** having a **density** equal to, or greater than 300 kg/m³ prior to avalanching.

Hazard, Avalanche—The potential for an avalanche(s) to cause damage to something of value. It is a combination of the likelihood of triggering and the destructive size of the avalanche(s). It implies the potential to affect people, facilities or things of value, but does not incorporate vulnerability or exposure to avalanches. Avalanche danger and hazard are synonymous and are commonly expressed using relative terms such as high, moderate and low.

Snow, Weather, and Avalanches

Heat—A form of energy associated with the motion of atoms or molecules that is capable of being transmitted through a solid by conduction, through fluid media by conduction and/or convection and through empty space by radiation.

Humidity—The amount of water vapor contained in air. Also see **relative humidity**.

Hysteresis— 1) The history dependence of physical systems. When the outcome of a physical process depends on the history of the element or the direction of the process. 2) The properties of an instrument that depend on approaching a point on the scale during a full-scale traverse in both directions.

Hysteretic Error—The difference between the upscale reading and downscale reading at any point on the scale obtained during a full-scale traverse. Also see **hysteresis**.

Incline—The steepness of a slope. The acute angle measured from the horizontal to the plane of a slope. Also termed **slope angle**.

Induced Errors—Errors that stem from equipment quality or deviation from a standard measurement technique.

Inherent Errors—Errors due to natural variations in the process of measurement and will vary in sign (+/-) and magnitude each time they occur.

Injured—A category of the avalanche toll for an accident. A person is considered injured if they require medical treatment after being **caught**, **partially buried-not critical**, **partially buried-critical**, or **completely buried** in an avalanche.

Isothermal—The state of equal temperature. In an isothermal snow cover there is no temperature gradient. Seasonal snow covers that are isothermal are typically 0°C.

Latent Heat—The quantity of heat absorbed or released by a substance undergoing a change of state, such as ice changing to water or water to steam, at constant **temperature** and **pressure**.

Layer, Snow—An element of a snow cover created by a weather, metamorphic, or other event.

Loose-Snow Avalanche—An avalanche that releases from a point and spreads downhill entraining snow. Also termed a **point-release avalanche** or a **sluff**.

Mitigation, Avalanche Hazard—To moderate the frequency, timing, force, or destructive effect of avalanches on people, property, or the environment through active or passive methods.

Mixing Ratio—The ratio of the mass of water vapor to the mass of dry air in a volume of air. The **mixing ratio** is dimensionless, but usually expressed as g/kg.

Partially Buried—Critical—A category of the avalanche toll for an accident. A person is *partially buried–critical* if their head is below the snow surface when the avalanche stops but equipment, clothing and/or portions of their body are visible.

Partially Buried—Not Critical—A category of the avalanche toll for an accident. A person is *partially buried–not critical* if their head was above the snow surface when the avalanche stops.

Partial Pressure—The **pressure** a component of a gaseous mixture would exert if it alone occupied the volume the entire mixture occupies.

Pendular, Wet Snow Regime—When continuous air spaces and discontinuous volumes of water exist in a snow cover. In a pendular snow cover: air-ice, water-ice and air-liquid connections exist simultaneously. It is generally assumed that snow with a liquid water content (by volume) of 3 – 8% is in the pendular regime. Also see the definition for the **funicular** regime.

Point-Release Avalanche—See **loose snow avalanche** or **sluff**.

Glossary

Precipitation Intensity—A measurement of the water equivalent that accumulated during a defined time period (usually 1 hour).

Precipitation Rate—An estimate of the amount of snow and/or rain that accumulated during a defined time period (usually 1 hour).

Precision—The level of detail that a measurement method can produce under identical conditions. Precision is a property of a measurement method and a measure of **repeatability**. The precision of a measurement method dictates the degree of discrimination with which a quantity is stated (i.e. a three digit numeral discriminates among 1,000 possibilities). Also see **accuracy**.

Pressure—The **force** applied to or distributed over a surface, measured as force per unit area. The International System of Units (SI) uses N/m^2 or a pascal (Pa) for pressure.

Relative Humidity—A dimensionless ratio of the **vapor pressure** to the **saturation vapor pressure**, or the **mixing ratio** to the **saturation mixing ratio**. Relative humidity is reported as percent (i.e. vapor pressure/ saturation vapor pressure x 100 = % relative humidity).

Remote Trigger—When an avalanche releases some distance away from the **trigger point**.

Repeatability—The difference between consecutive measurements obtained by the same measurement method under the same conditions.

Resolution—The smallest interval between two adjacent, discrete measured values that can be distinguished from each other under specified conditions.

Return Period—The average time interval between occurrences of an event of given or greater magnitude. Usually expressed in years.

Risk— The chance of something happening that will have an impact on an element (person, vehicle, structure, etc…). A risk is often specified in terms of an event or circumstance and the consequences that may follow. Risk is evaluated in terms of a combination of the consequences of an event and their likelihood.

Running Surface—The surface over which an avalanche flows below the **stauchwall**. This surface can extend from the **stauchwall**, through the **track**, and into the **runout zone**. The running surface can be composed of one or more snowpack layers.

Runout Zone—The portion of an avalanche path where the avalanche **debris** typically comes to rest due to a decrease in **slope angle**, a natural obstacle, or loss of momentum.

Saturation Mixing Ratio—The **mixing ratio** of a parcel of air that is at equilibrium. See definitions of **vapor pressure, saturation vapor pressure** and **equilibrium vapor pressure**.

Saturation Vapor Pressure—The **partial pressure** of a vapor when **evaporation** and **condensation** are occurring at the same rate over a flat surface of pure substance (i.e. water). The saturation vapor pressure is a special case of the **equilibrium vapor pressure**.

Sensitivity—The response of a measurement method to a change in the parameter being measured. The sensitivity of a measurement method is usually expressed as a ratio. Example: For a mercury thermometer the sensitivity equals the change in length of the column of mercury per degree of temperature (m/°C).

Settling, Settlement—The slow, internal deformation and densification of snow under the influence of gravity. A component of **creep**.

SI Units—Système International d'Unités. An international system of units. See Appendix B.

Slab—A cohesive snowpack element consisting of one or more snow **layers**.

Snow, Weather, and Avalanches

Slab Avalanche—An avalanche that releases a cohesive **slab** of snow producing a **fracture line**.

Slope Angle —The acute angle measured from the horizontal to the plane of a slope.

Sluff—A **loose snow avalanche** or **point release avalanche**.

Snow Profile—A pit dug vertically into the snowpack where observations of snow cover stratigraphy and characteristics of the individual layers are observed. Also used to describe data collected by this method at an individual site.

Soft Slab—A snow **slab** with a **density** less than 300 kg/m³.

Spatial Variability—The variation of physical properties across the physical extent, or various spatial scales, of a material. Typical scales in snow avalanche research and practice include the continental scale (defining variations in snow and avalanche climates), the regional scale (such as regions covered by backcountry avalanche advisories), the scale of individual mountain ranges (of various sizes), and the scale of individual slopes. Physical properties investigated vary, but include weak layer shear strength, stability test scores, penetration resistance, microstructural parameters, layer continuity, snow water equivalent, snow depth, and other characteristics.

Stability—1) A property of a system where the effects of an induced disturbance decrease in magnitude and the system returns to its original state. 2) For avalanche forecasting stability is the chance that avalanches do not initiate. Stability is analyzed in space and time relative to a given triggering level or load.

Starting Zone—The portion of an **avalanche path** from where the avalanche releases.

Stauchwall—The downslope fracture surface of a **slab avalanche**.

Strain—The deformation of a physical body under an external **force** represented by a dimensionless ratio (m/m).

Strength—1) The ability of a material to resist **strain** or **stress**. 2) The maximum **stress** a snow layer can withstand without failing or fracturing.

Stress—The distribution of force over a particular area. Expressed in units of **force** per area (N/m²).

Study Plot—A fixed location where atmospheric and snow properties are measured and recorded. Study plot locations are chosen to limit the effects of external influences (i.e. wind, sun, slope angle) and are typically close to level.

Study Slope—A fixed, normally inclined location where snow properties and snow **stability** are measured and recorded. Atmospheric fields can also be recorded at a study slope. Study slope locations are chosen in relatively uniform areas, so that snow properties can be monitored over time and extrapolated to **starting zones**.

Sublimation—Strictly defined as the conversion of mass between solid and gas phases due to changes in **temperature** and/or **pressure**. Commonly used to describe mass conversion from solid to gas, with **deposition** describing a phase change in the opposite direction.

Sympathetic Trigger—When an avalanche triggers another avalanche some distance away. The second avalanche releases due to the disturbance of the first.

Targeted Site—A location where a targeted observation is conducted. A targeted site is chosen to investigate parameters of interest to a particular observer at a particular location. Data from targeted sites complements data from **study plots** and **study slopes**.

Glossary

Temperature—Often defined as the condition of a body that determines the transfer of **heat** to or from other bodies. Particularly, it is a manifestation of the average translational kinetic energy of the molecules of a substance due to heat agitation. Also, the degree of hotness or coldness measured on a definite scale.

Temperature Gradient—The change in **temperature** over a distance. Expressed in units of degrees per length (i.e. °C/m).

Test Profile—A snow profile where selected characteristics of the snowpack are observed and recorded. **Stability** tests are typically conducted in a **test profile**. Also see **full profile**.

Track—The portion of an avalanche path that lies below the **starting zone** and above the **runout zone**.

Trigger—The mechanism that increases the load on the snowpack, or changes its physical properties to the point that **fracture** and subsequent avalanching occurs.

Trigger Point—The area where a **trigger** is applied.

Vapor Pressure—The **partial pressure** of a vapor.

Vulnerability— The degree to which an exposed element (person, vehicle, structure, etc…) will suffer loss from the impact of a specific natural hazard.

Wind Sensor—An instrument that measures both wind speed and direction.

Wind Slab—A dense layer(s) of snow formed by wind deposition.

Whumpf—See **collapse**

Snow, Weather, and Avalanches

Appendix A
References

A.1 References Cited

Birkeland, K., and R. Johnson, 1999: The stuffblock snow stability test: comparability with the rutschblock usefulness in different snow climates and repeatability between observers. *Cold Regions Science and Technology*, **30**, 115-123.

Birkeland, K., and R. Johnson, 2003: Integrating shear quality into stability test results. *The Avalanche News*, **67**, 30-35.

Dennis, A., and M. Moore, 1996: Evolution of public avalanche information: The North American experience with avalanche danger rating levels. *Proceedings of the International Snow Science Workshop*, Banff, British Columbia, October, 1996, 60-72.

Föhn, P.M.B., 1987a: The rutschblock as a practical tool for slope stability evaluation. *Avalanche Formation, Movement, and Effects*, B. Salm and H. Gubler, (eds.), IAHS-AISH Publication No. 162, 223-228.

Föhn, P.M.B., 1987b: The stability index and various triggering mechanisms. *Avalanche Formation, Movement, and Effects*, B. Salm and H. Gubler, (eds.), IAHS-AISH Publication No. 162, 195-211.

Canadian Avalanche Association, 2002: *Observational Guidelines and Recording Standards for Weather Snowpack, and Avalanches*. Canadian Avalanche Association, Revelstoke, 78 pp.

Colbeck, S., and others, 1990: *The International Classification for Seasonal Snow on the Ground*. International Commission on Snow and Ice (IAHS), World Data Center A for Glaciology, University of Colorado, Boulder, Colorado, 23 pp.

Gauthier, D., and B. Jamieson. 2007. Evaluation of a prototype field test for fracture and failure propagation propensity in weak snowpack layers, *Cold Regions Science and Technology*, doi:10.1016/j.coldregions.2007.04.005

Gauthier, D., Jamieson, J.B., 2008. Fracture propagation propensity in relation to snow slab avalanche release: validating the propagation saw test. Geophys. Res. Lett. 35 (L13501). doi:10.1029/2008GL034245.

Hendrikx, J. and K.W. Birkeland. 2008. Slope scale spatial variability across time and space: Comparison of results from two different snow climates. *Proceedings of the 2008 International Snow Science Workshop*, Whistler, British Columbia, Canada.

Jamieson, B., 1996: Avalanche prediction for persistent snow slabs. Ph.D. dissertation, Department of Civil Engineering, University of Calgary, Calgary, Alberta. 255 pp.

Jamieson, B., 1996: The compression test – after 25 years. *The Avalanche Review*, **18**, 10-12.

Jamieson, J.B., and C.D. Johnston, 1993: Experience with rutschblocks. *Proceedings of the International Snow Science Workshop*, Breckenridge, Colorado, October 1992, 150-159.

Jamieson, J.B., and C.D. Johnston, 1993: Rutschblock precision, technique variations and limitations. *Journal of Glaciology*, **39**, 666-674.

Jamieson, J.B., and C.D. Johnston, 2001: Evaluation of the shear frame test for weak snowpack layers. *Annals of Glaciology*, **32**, 59-66.

Jamieson, J.B., and J. Schweizer, 2000: Texture and strength changes of buried surface hoar layers with implications for dry snow-slab avalanche release. *Journal of Glaciology*, **46**, 151-160.

Johnson, B.C., J.B. Jamieson, and C.D. Johnston, 2000: Field studies of the cantilever beam test. *The Avalanche Review* **18**, 8-9.

Appendix A: References

Johnson, R., and K. Birkeland, 1998: Effectively using and interpreting stability tests. *Proceedings of the International Snow Science Workshop*, Sunriver, Oregon, October 1998, 562-565.

Johnson, R., and K. Birkeland, 2002: Integrating shear quality into stability test results. *Proceedings of the International Snow Science Workshop*, Penticton, British Columbia, October 2002, 508-513.

LaChapelle, E. R., 1992: *Field Guide to Snow Crystals*. International Glaciological Society, Cambridge, 86 pp.

Lied, K. and S. Bakkehøi, 1980: Empirical calculations of snow-avalanche runout distance based on topographic parameters, *Journal of Glaciology*, **26**, 165–177.

McClung, D.M., and P. Schaerer, 1981: Snow avalanche size classification. *Proceedings of Avalanche Workshop 1980*, National Research Council, Associate Committee on Geotechnical Research; Technical Memorandum No. 133, 12-27.

McClung, D.M., and P. Schaerer, 1993: *The Avalanche Handbook*. The Mountaineers (pub), Seattle, 271 pp.

McClung, D.M., A. Mears, and P. Schaerer, 1989: Extreme avalanche runout: data from four mountain ranges. *Annals of Glaciology*, **13**, 180-184.

Mears, A., 1992: *Snow Avalanche Hazard Analysis for Land-use Planning and Engineering*. Colorado Geological Survey Bulletin No. 49, Denver, CO.

Mears, A., 1998: Tensile strength and strength changes in new snow layers. *Proceedings of the International Snow Science Workshop*, Sunriver, Oregon, 574-576.

Moner, I. J. Gavaldà, M. Bacardit, C. Garcia and G. Martí. 2008. Application of the Field Stability Evaluation Methods to the Snow Conditions of the Eastern Pyrenees. *Proceedings of the 2008 International Snow Science Workshop*, Whistler, British Columbia, Canada.

Perla, R.I., 1969: Strength tests on newly fallen snow. *Journal of Glaciology,* **8**, 427-440.

Perla, R.I., 1978: Snow Crystals/Les Cristaux de Neige; National Hydrology Research Institute, Paper No. 1, Ottawa, 19 pp.

Perla, R.I., 1980: Avalanche Release, Motion, and Impact. *Dynamics of Snow and Ice Masses*. S.C. Colbeck (ed.), Academic Press, New York, 397-462.

Perla, R.I., and M. Martinelli, Jr., 1976 (Revised 1978): *Avalanche Handbook*. United States Department of Agriculture, Forest Service; Agriculture Handbook No. 489, Washington, D.C., 238 pp.

Roch, A., 1966: Les variations de la resistence de la neige. *Proceedings of the International Symposium on Scientific Aspects of Snow and Ice Avalanches*. Gentbrugge, Belgium, IAHS Publication, 182-195.

Schweizer, J., 2002: The rutschblock test: procedures and application in Switzerland. *Avalanche Review,* **20**, 14-15.

Schweizer, J., K. Kronholm, J.B. Jamieson, and K.W. Birkeland. 2008: Review of spatial variability of snowpack properties and its importance for avalanche formation. *Cold Regions Science and Technology* 51, 253-272.

Sigrist, C., 2006. Measurement of Fracture Mechanical Properties of Snow and Application to Dry Snow Slab Avalanche Release. Ph.D. Thesis, Swiss Federal Institute of Technology, Zurich., 139pp.

Simenhois, R. and K.W. Birkeland. 2007. An update on the Extended Column Test: New recording standards and additional data analyses. *The Avalanche Review* 26(2).

Simenhois, R. and K.W. Birkeland. 2006. The extended column test: A field test for fracture initiation and propagation. *Proceedings of the 2006 International Snow Science Workshop*, Telluride, Colorado.

Simenhois, R., Birkeland, K.W. 2009: The Extended Column Test: Test effectiveness, spatial variability, and comparison with the Propagation Saw Test, *Cold Regions Science and Technology*, doi:10.1016/j.coldregions.2009.04.001

Sterbenz, C., 1998: The cantilever beam or "Bridgeblock" snow strength test. *Proceedings of the International Snow Science Workshop,* Sunriver, Oregon, 566-573.

van Herwijnen, A., and B. Jamieson, 2002: Interpreting fracture character in stability tests. *Proceedings of the International Snow Science Workshop*, Penticton, British Columbia, 514-520.

van Herwijnen, A., and B. Jamieson, 2003: An update on fracture character in stability tests. *Avalanche News,* **66**, 26-28.

Winkler, K., and J. Schweizer, 2009:Comparison of snow stability tests: Extended column test, rutschblock test and compression test, *Cold Regions Science and Technology.*, doi:10.1016/j.coldregions.2009.05.003

World Meteorological Organization (WMO), 1996: *Guide to Meteorological Instruments and Methods of Observation.* WMO Publication No. 8, Geneva, Switzerland. (WMO documents can be obtained from the American Meteorological Society www.ametsoc.org)

A.2   Other Useful References

Snow and Avalanche Climatology

Armstrong, R., and B. Armstrong, 1987: Snow and avalanche climates in the western United States. B. Salm and H. Gubler, (eds.), IAHS-AISH Publication No. 162, 281-294.

Mock, C.J., and K.W. Birkeland, 2000: Snow avalanche climatology of the western United States Mountain Ranges. *Bulletin of the American Meteorological Society*, **81**, 2367-2392.

Instruments and Methods

Brock, F.V., and S.J. Richardson, 2001: *Meteorological Measurement Systems.* Oxford University Press, New York, 290 pp.

Doesken, N.J., and A. Judson, 1996: *The Snow Booklet – A guide to science, climatology, and measurement of snow in the United States.* Colorado Climate Center, Department of Atmospheric Science, Colorado State University, 86 pp.

Sevruk, B., and L. Zahlavova, 1994: Classification system of precipitation gauge site exposure: evaluation and application. *International Journal of Climatology,* **14**, 681-689.

Avalanche Forecasting

LaChapell, E.R., 1966: Avalanche forecasting—A modern synthesis. International Association of Hydrological Sciences, Publication No. 69, 350-356.

LaChapelle, E.R., 1980: The fundamental processes in conventional avalanche forecasting. *Journal of Glaciology*, **26**, 75-84.

McClung, D.M., 2002: The elements of applied avalanche forecasting, Part 1: The human issues. *Natural Hazards,* **26**, 111-129.

McClung, D.M., 2002: The elements of applied avalanche forecasting, Part 2: The physical issues and the rules of applied avalanche forecasting. *Natural Hazards,* **26**, 111-129.

Perla, R.I., 1970: On the contributory factors in avalanche hazard evaluation. *Canadian Geotechnical Journal,* **7**, 414-419.

Land Management

Weir, P., 2002: Snow avalanche management in forested terrain. Research Branch, British Columbia Ministry of Forestry, Victoria, B.C. Land Management Handbook No. 55. (available at www.for.gov.bc.ca/hfd/pubs/Docs/Lmh/Lmh55.htm), pp. 190.

Appendix B
Units

B.1 Units

A unit is a particular physical quantity, defined and adopted by convention, to which other quantities of the same kind are compared to determine their relative value. The use of a common system of units aids in communication of quantities, qualities, and rules of thumb between people and programs. A recommended system of units for snow, weather, and avalanche observations is listed in section B.2. It follows the International System of Units (SI) (section B.3) with a few exceptions.

B.2 Units for Snow, Weather and Avalanche Observations

In the United States, personnel of avalanche operations and users of their products may not be familiar with all SI units. For this reason individual programs should choose a unit system that suits their particular application. Data records generated for regional and national databases should use the international units listed below (or clearly list units used in accompanying metadata files). Deviations from the international units should use the common U.S. units listed below. Conversions between the two systems are listed in section B.4.

Table B.1 Recommended Units for Snow, Weather, and Avalanche Observations

Quantity	International Unit		Common U.S. Unit	
	Unit	Symbol	Unit	Symbol
temperature — air	degree Celsius	°C	degree Fahrenheit	°F
temperature — snow	degree Celsius	°C	degree Celsius	°C
wind speed	meter/second	m/s	mile/hour	mi/hr
aspect and wind direction	compass degree	°	compass direction	N,NE,E,SE, S,SW,W,NW
relative humidity	percent water	%	percent water	%
barometric pressure	millibar	mb (1 mb = 1 hPa)	inches of mercury	inHg
new snow depth	centimeter	cm	inch	in
total snow depth	centimeter or meter	cm or m	inch	in
water equivalent of precipitation or snowpack	millimeter	mm	inch	in
density	kilogram/cubic meter	kg/m^3	percent water	%
snow grain size	millimeter	mm	millimeter	mm
length	meter	m	foot	ft

Note: Most topographic maps in North America use feet as the unit for elevation. Thus it is more practical to use feet for the common elevation unit. Field observations can use feet to record elevations, however metadata for weather and snow study plots should list the elevation in meters.

Snow, Weather, and Avalanches

B.3   SI Units

The Système International d'Unités (SI), or International System of Units, has been accepted by most of the nations of the world as a common language for science and industry. It defines a set of base units from which other quantities are derived. Details of the International System of Units can be found at http://physics.nist.gov/cuu/Units/. Common conversion factors are listed in section B.4.

Some derived SI units have been given special names to make them easier to use.

For large or small quantities, a set of prefixes and associated decimal multiples can be used with SI units. These prefixes can be used with any base or derived SI unit with the exception of kilogram. Since the base unit kilogram already contains the prefix kilo, the set of prefixes are used with the unit name gram.

Example of prefix use:

$1 \text{ m} \times 10^3 = 1 \text{ kilometer}$
$1 \text{ m} \times 1000 = 1 \text{ kilometer}$
$1 \text{ kilometer} = 1000 \text{ m}$

Table B.2 SI Base Units

Quantity	Unit Name	Unit Symbol
length	meter	m
mass	kilogram	kg
time	second	s
temperature	kelvin	K
amount of substance	mole	mol
electric current	ampere	A
luminous intensity	candela	cd

Table B.3 Common Derived SI Units

Quantity	Unit Name	Unit Symbol
area	square meter	m^2
volume	cubic meter	m^3
speed	meter per second	m/s
acceleration	meter per second squared	m/s^2
density	kilogram per cubic meter	kg/m^3

Appendix B: Units

Table B.4 Derived SI Units with Special Names

Quantity	Unit Name	Unit Symbol	Derived Definition	Base Definition
force	newton	N		$kg{\times}m/s^2$
pressure or stress	pascal	Pa	N/m^2	$kg/(m{\times}s^2)$
energy or work	joule	J	$N{\times}m$	$kg{\times}m^2/s^2$
power	watt	W	J/s	$kg{\times}m^2/s^3$
Celsius temperature	degree Celsius	°C		K
plane angle	radian	rad		m/m

Table B.5 SI Unit Prefixes

Factor	Name	Symbol
10^{12}	tera	T
10^{9}	giga	G
10^{6}	mega	M
10^{3}	kilo	k
10^{2}	hecto	h
10^{-2}	centi	c
10^{-3}	milli	m
10^{-6}	micro	m
10^{-9}	nano	n
10^{-12}	pico	p

B.4   Conversion Tables
B.4.1   Unit Analysis

Unit conversions can be accomplished by a method known as *unit analysis*. Each unit can be written as a combination of base units, such as length, time, or mass. Then conversion can be accomplished by multiplying by a unit ratio, canceling the unwanted units and thus leaving the desired value. This technique combined with the use of the SI unit prefixes can be used to accomplish most conversions.

Example:

$$5.0 \ m \times \frac{3.28 \ ft}{1 \ m} = 16.4 \ ft$$

$$5.0 \ \frac{mi}{hr} \times \frac{5,280 \ ft}{1 \ mi} \times \frac{1 \ m}{3.28 \ ft} \times \frac{1 \ hr}{3600 \ s} = 2.2 \ \frac{m}{s}$$

$$20.67 \ inHg \times 3386.389 \ ^* \frac{Pa}{inHg} \cong 70,000 \ Pa \times \frac{1 \ bar}{100,000 \ Pa} = 0.7 \ bar \times \frac{1000 \ mb}{bar} = 700 \ mb$$

*This is a conversion for inches of mercury at 0°C

The appropriate ratios can be easily constructed if you know the proper proportions.

Example:

There are 5,280 feet in 1 mile → $\dfrac{5{,}280\ \text{ft}}{1\ \text{mi}}$

There are 60 seconds in 1 minute → $\dfrac{60\ \text{s}}{1\ \text{min}}$

B.4.2 Time

There are:

60 seconds in 1 minute
60 minutes in 1 hour
24 hours in 1 day
365 days in 1 year (366 days in one leap year)

B.4.3 Temperature

For temperature conversions it is more appropriate to list conversion equations.

$°C = K - 273.15$ $K = °C + 273.15$

$°C = (5/9)(°F - 32)$ $°F = (9/5)°C + 32$

B.4.4 Speed

1 mi/hr = 1.609344 km/hr   1 m/s = 3.6 km/hr
       = 0.8689762 knots   = 2.2369363 mi/hr
       = 0.44704 m/s   = 1.9438445 knots

1 km/hr = 0.6213712 mi/hr   1 knot = 1.1507794 mi/hr
       = 0.2777778 m/s   = 0.514444 m/s
       = 0.5399568 knots   = 1.852 km/hr

B.4.5 Pressure

1 Pa = 0.00001 bar
      = 0.01 mb = 0.01 hPa
      = 0.000295 inches of mercury at 0°C
      = 0.007501 millimeters of mercury at 0°C
      = 0.000009869 atm

B.4.6 Length

1 in = 2.54 cm
1 ft = 0.3048 m
1 mi = 1609.344 m

B.4.7 Density

The density of snow is usually calculated by weighing a sample of known volume.

Example:

If the mass of a 250 cm^3 snow sample is 70 g, then:

$$\frac{70\text{g}}{250\text{cm}^3} = 0.28\,\frac{\text{g}}{\text{cm}^3} \times \frac{1\text{kg}}{1000\text{g}} \times \frac{1{,}000{,}000\text{cm}^3}{1\text{m}^3} = 280\,\frac{\text{kg}}{\text{m}^3}$$

Appendix B: Units

Simple relations can be determined for common calculations. For example if you typically use a 250 cm³ cutter to take your snow sample then you can multiply the mass in grams by 4 to obtain the density in kg/m³.

The percent water content of a snow sample is often communicated as a dimensionless ratio or percent. It is easily calculated by dividing the density of the snow by the density of water (1000 kg/m³) and multiplying by one hundred. Using the density of water allows for an easy calculation by moving the decimal one space to the left (ie: 280 kg/m³ = 28%).

The percent water content of a snow sample can also be obtained by dividing the height of its water equivalent by the height of the snow layer and then multipling by 100.

Example:

If you have 10 cm of snow whose water equivalent is 1 cm of water.

$$\frac{1\,(cm)\,water}{10\,(cm)\,snow} = 0.1 \times 100 = 10\%\ water\ content$$

B.5   Expanded Equations

Several equations are presented in abbreviated form in the text. The expanded versions below are intended to explain how the abbreviated versions were derived.

Section 1.22

$$H2DW\ (mm)\ =\ \frac{mass\ of\ snow\ sample\ (g)}{area\ of\ snow\ sample\ (cm^2)} \times 10$$

Expanded Equation

$$H2DW\ (mm) = \frac{mass\ (g)}{area\ (cm^2)} \times \frac{1\,(cm^2)}{100\,(mm^2)} \times \frac{1\,(cm^3\ of\ water)}{1(g\ of\ water)} \times \frac{1000\,(mm^3)}{1\,(cm^3)}$$

Section 1.23

$$\rho\left(\frac{kg}{m^3}\right) = \frac{mass\ of\ snow\ sample(g)}{sample\ volume\ (cm^3)} \times 1000$$

Expanded Equation

$$\rho\left(\frac{kg}{m^3}\right) = \frac{mass\ of\ snow\ sample\ (g)}{sample\ volume\ (cm^3)} \times \frac{1,000,000\ (cm^3)}{1\,(m^3)} \times \frac{1\,(kg)}{1000\ (g)}$$

Section 1.23

$$\rho\left(\frac{kg}{m^3}\right) = \frac{H2DW\ (mm)}{H2D\ (cm)} \times 100$$

Expanded Equation

$$\rho\left(\frac{kg}{m^3}\right) = \frac{water\ equiv.\ of\ snow\ sample\ (mm)}{height\ of\ snow\ sample\ (cm)} \times \frac{1\,(cm)}{10\,(mm)} \times \frac{1(g\ water)}{1(cm^3\ water)} \times \frac{1\,(kg)}{1000\ (g)} \times \frac{1,000,000(cm^3)}{1(m^3)}$$

Appendix C
Metadata

C.1 Introduction

Metadata is information about data (data about data). It is an integral part of maintaining a long-term record. Metadata provides a chronology of methods used to obtain a dataset and can provide important information for observers and data users alike.

C.2 File Format and Content

There is no clear method for collecting and recording metadata. What should be recorded and how to record it depends on the application. For avalanche operations we recommend maintaining a "field book" for each observation site. This field book could be an actual book stored at the site or an electronic or paper file stored in an office. An example of commonly recorded metadata fields for a meteorological site are listed in section C.3

A metadata file should contain a basic description of the observation site. This includes, but is not limited to, location, aspect, elevation and exposure. A photographic record of the site and changes to the site may be useful. A description of each instrument should be included. Metadata files should also contain a record of site maintenance and instrument calibration; and a list of measurements made at the site should be in the order that they are listed in the record or data file. Data is assumed to be in the recommended system of international units listed in Appendix B unless other units are specified in the metadata file. Metadata and data archives should be stored as comma delimited text files or Microsoft Excel files.

C.3 Metadata Example for Meteorological Observation Sites

1) Site
   a. Station/site name/site ID
   b. Lock combination
   c. Lat / Lon (map datum: NAD27 or NAD83/ WSG84) or UTM
   d. Elevation
   e. Aspect
   f. Slope angle
   g. Photographs from each aspect
   h. Changes to site (date and type)
   i. Comments
2) Operation Status
   a. Year-round
   b. Seasonal
   c. Special
   d. Start date
   e. End date
3) Type
   a. Study plot
   b. Mountaintop
   c. Ridgetop
4) Power
   a. None
   b. Solar/battery
   c. AC
5) Sensors
   a. Properties
      i. Make
      ii. Model
      iii. Serial Number
      iv. Type
   b. Installation
      i. Height above ground
      ii. Distance from tower or obstacle
      iii. Date installed
      iv. Sampling rate
      v. Average length and technique
      vi. Service and calibration dates
      vii. Units of stored values
      viii. Comments

6) Data Loggers
   a. Brand
   b. Model
   c. Serial Number
   d. Type
   e. Acquisition date
   f. Service dates
   g. Comments
7) Data Retrieval
   a. Direct – manual
   b. Radio telemetry
   c. Cellular phone
   d. Telephone
   e. Short haul modem
   f. Satellite
8) Software
   a. Product name
   b. Version number
   c. Program name
   d. Installation date
   e. Upgrade date
   f. Comments
9) Observer Contact Information
   a. Name
   b. Agency
   c. Address
   d. Telephone
   e. Email

Snow, Weather, and Avalanches

Appendix D
Observation Sites for Meteorological Measurements

D.1 Introduction

Measurements of precipitation, temperature, wind, and the characteristics of the snowpack are dependent on the observation site. The utmost care must be taken to select a site for weather and/or snowpack observations that is geographically representative of the forecast area or avalanche starting zones. Measurements made at study sites often serve as baseline information from which conditions in starting zones can be extrapolated.

Site selection requires knowledge of the area and skill in meeting contradictory needs. Sometimes parallel observations may be recorded in several possible locations for one winter before a permanent site is chosen, or a site may have to be abandoned after yielding unsatisfactory correlations. The access should be convenient and safe under normal conditions.

Site characteristics differ depending on the parameter of interest and the application of the data. Avalanche forecasting operations typically require precipitation measurements from sheltered locations and wind measurements in exposed areas. For this reason more than one observation site may be necessary for an individual program. Ideally each program would have at least one site where all of the basic meteorological parameters are observed, and one or more sites where at least wind speed, wind direction, and air temperature are measured.

The guidelines presented in this appendix represent the best-case scenario. Some of the guidelines will be difficult for all avalanche forecasting operations to achieve. These guidelines should be considered during the site selection process, before a practical site is selected.

Figure D.1 A remote weather station at a valley bottom site (photograph by Billy Rankin).

D.2 Meteorological and Snowpack Study Site Selection

Observation sites should be selected so that measurements made at the site will be representative of the forecast area. The site should be as close as possible to avalanche starting zones and still permit regular observations. Exposure issues usually dictate separate sites for wind and precipitation measurements. When separate sites are deemed necessary, air temperature measurements should be collected from both sites.

A meteorological study site will ideally be located in a level, open area that is devoid of large vegetation. The World Meteorological Organization (WMO) recommends a site 10 meters by 7 meters (WMO, 1996). This recommendation should be treated as an ideal, as significantly smaller sites may be more appropriate for observations in exposed mountain areas. The surface should be cleared so that the ground cover consists of short grass or the predominate ground cover in the area. Instruments should be placed in a measurement site (approximately two-meter by two-meter area) at the center of the opening. A visual barrier or signs should surround the area to prevent unwary travelers from disturbing the study site.

Snowpack observation sites can be co-located with meteorological sites if adequate space is available. Snowpack and precipitation measurement sites should be sheltered from the wind. Sites that minimize snow drifting should be selected if wind effects cannot be avoided. The main requirement for wind stations is a good correlation between measurements at observation locations and avalanche starting zones.

Figure D.2 The Utah Department of Transportation's study site in Alta, Utah (photograph by Bruce Tremper).

Appendix D: Observational Sites for Meteorological Observations

D.3 Instrument Exposure

Precipitation

For sites where precipitation measurements are made, it is recommended that the instrument (snow board, rain gauge, snow depth sensor, etc.) be at least as far from the nearest obstacle (building, tree, fence post, etc.) as that obstacle is high. Precipitation sites should be devoid of sloping terrain if possible and away from depressions or hollows. Rooftop sites should be avoided. When practical or environmental constraints require deviating from these guidelines, the changes can be recorded in the metadata file (see Appendix C).

Precipitation gauges located at windy sites can seriously underestimate the actual precipitation amount. Gauge catch can be improved by the following methods listed in the order of effectiveness (WMO, 1996):

1) The vegetation height of the site can be maintained at the same height as the gauge orifice, thus maintaining a horizontal wind flow over the gauge.
2) The effect listed in point 1 can be simulated by an artificial structure (i.e. fence).
3) The use of a wind shield such as an Alter or Neipher shield, or a similar device around the gauge orifice.

Many avalanche operations use ultra-sonic distance instruments to remotely monitor snow height. These gauges can be used to record both total snow height (HN) or interval values (e.g. HN24). The response of these instruments is affected by both air temperature (which can be addressed in the datalogger program) and the concentration of airborne particles.

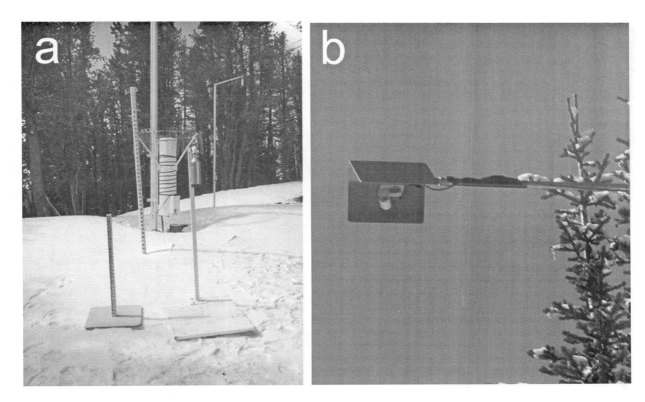

Figure D.3 Two examples of precipitation instrument installations. a) A comprehensive precipitation site with a total precipitation gauge, as well as total and interval snow height (manual and automated measurements) (photograph by Tom Leonard). b) An ultra-sonic distance sensor modified for a site subject to large snowfall events (photograph by Mark Moore).

105

Temperature

Temperature instruments must be properly ventilated and sheltered from radiation sources. This can be accomplished by housing the instrument in a commercial radiation shield or Stevenson screen. Manual and automated instruments can be co-located in a Stevenson screen. The screen door should open to the north to prevent solar heating of the temperature sensors.

Temperature instruments should be located 1.25 m to 2 m above the surface (WMO, 1996). Ideally the instrument shelter is mounted on an adjustable post so that a constant distance above the surface can be maintained. The instrument should be exposed to wind and sun (although properly shielded). Depressions or hollows that can trap cold air should be avoided. Temperature measurements should not be made near buildings or on rooftops.

Relative Humidity

Instrument exposure issues for relative humidity measurements will depend on the measurement method. Relative humidity measurements in below freezing environments can be difficult and instrument selection is critical (and beyond the scope of this discussion). In general, instruments should be sheltered from direct solar radiation, atmospheric contaminants, precipitation and wind (WMO, 1996). Materials such as wood and some synthetic products can absorb and desorb water according to atmospheric humidity (WMO, 1996). If the enclosure is made of wood it should be coated in white enamel paint (creating a vapor barrier). Relative humidity instruments can be co-located with temperature instruments provided that these issues are addressed.

Wind

Anemometers should ideally be located atop a vibration-free, 10-meter (~30 ft) tower. Wind measurements can be dramatically affected by the presence of upstream obstacles. Ideally, there should be no obstructions within a 100 m (~ 300 ft) radius of the anemometer (WMO, 1996). In mountainous terrain, where large obstacles are prevalent, anemometers at two or more locations can be used to gain adequate wind information in a variety of conditions. Local obstructions, such as the tower or other instruments, should be a distance away from the wind sensor that is four to five times the diameter of the

Figure D.4 Two examples of automated wind sites. a) An exposed site to monitor general atmospheric flow (photograph by Mark Moore). b) Wind and temperature instruments at multiple levels to monitor vertical variations in atmospheric conditions. This site also include instrumentation to monitor solar and terrestrial radiation (photograph by Kelly Elder).

obstruction. These effects can be addressed by placing the wind sensor atop of the tower.

Several wind stations may be needed to obtain a reasonable feel for wind effects within a forecast area. Considerable separation (vertical and horizontal) may be required to achieve a suitable representation of the actual wind field. It is essential that cup anemometers be horizontal to the underlying surface. All stations must be accessible in the winter either by foot, snowmobile or helicopter for occasional maintenance of equipment. Rime ice accretion is a common problem that can be addressed with heated sensors.

Radiation

Radiation processes have a large effect on snowpack stability and avalanche release. Instrument exposure issues will depend on the type of radiation measured and the direction of the radiation (incoming or outgoing), but radiation can be measured at any study site. If only one radiation component can be measured, incoming shortwave radiation may be the most useful. However, both short and longwave components can benefit avalanche applications.

Incoming shortwave radiation can be measured in a flat open area. Sensors should be installed so that they are level and in locations that are not in the shadow of buildings, trees, and when possible mountains. Shadowing should be evaluated throughout the day and season for instrument placement. The effects of the tower will be minimized if the instrument is placed a significant distance from (long arm) and on the south side (in the Northern Hemisphere) of the tower. It may also be beneficial to place incoming shortwave sensors above the vegetation canopy.

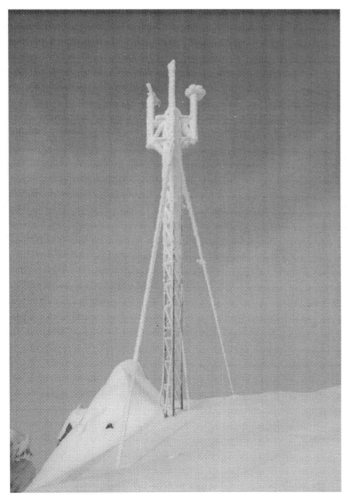

Figure D.5 A weather station coated in rime ice (photograph by John Stimberis).

Snow, Weather, and Avalanches

Appendix E
Automated Weather Stations

E.1 Introduction

Automated measurements of snow and weather phenomena are extremely useful components of an observational record. Automated sites provide an uninterrupted record and yield information about areas that are not commonly visited. Automated measurements allow observers to fill in the periods between manual observations, and may provide key information that would otherwise be missed. In many cases it may be more practical to maintain a weather record that is a combination of manual and automated measurements. When possible, automated measurements should be used to augment and not replace manual observations.

E.2 Objectives

The purpose of this appendix is to:

- Establish common methods for recording and reporting data collected by automated stations
- Encourage uniformity of measurements
- Provide methods for combining manual and automated data
- Encourage methods that produce data that is compatible with other long-term records.

E.3 Combining Manual and Automated Data

Maintaining a separate manual and automated data record is generally preferred. Replacing manual observations with automated measurements should only be employed when the operation headquarters are a significant distance from the avalanche terrain, or if access to a study site is unreliable.

Daily weather summaries that include a combination of manual observations and automated measurements are often useful for operations that make decisions based on these data. This practice is not a problem until the data set is transmitted to another user or central database. Manual and automated records can be co-located as long as a careful record of the source and type of measurement is present in the metadata file (see Appendix C). However, maintaining separate manual and automated data records is recommended.

The most common parameters obtained from automated weather stations are wind speed, wind direction, and temperature. Automated measurements of precipitation and total snow depth have become more common with improvements in sensors. Automated depth sensors can be used to record valuable interval measurements at stations that can not be visited regularly.

Values for wind speed and direction for daily observation sheets can be obtained by recording the hourly average from the period during which the manual observations were made. Maximum and minimum temperatures can also be obtained from an automated station provided that system explicitly records these values. The 24-hour maximum and minimum temperature should be averages of a period no longer than one minute (WMO, 1996).

E.4 Sampling Rates and Averaging Periods

The time interval between measurements (sampling rate) is an important and complex issue. Avalanche forecasting operations typically use a sampling rate of 3 to 5 seconds for temperature, wind, relative humidity, and pressure measurements. However, longer execution intervals (up to 60 sec) may be necessary at remote stations where power is limited. Precipitation measurement rates will depend on the instrument. Snow depth sensors can be sampled at the same rate that data is stored (i.e. 10 minute, 1 hour, etc.). Other precipitation sensors may require the computation of a running total rather than an average. These are practical solutions that work for many applications. Operations that require more robust sampling schemes are referred to World Meteorological Organization Publication Number 8 (see Appendix A for full reference).

Power constraints may dictate sampling schemes in remote locations. If these issues prevent continuous sampling, measurements can be sampled for 5 minutes before the hour and data can be recorded and reported on the hour.

The period over which a parameter is averaged depends upon the application. Many avalanche forecasting operations find it useful to look at averages of 5, 10, or 15 minute periods. These short interval averages will be most useful during storm periods, while one-hour averages are more useful for daily operations. Parameters stored in six-hour averages will conform to other long-term records such as climatic datasets. It is recommended that one-hour averages be stored as the long-term record.

Most parameters measured at automated weather stations can be averaged with a simple scheme. Wind direction is the most notable exception. Wind direction averages must be computed with a scheme that accounts for the circular nature of the values. Most data logger programming structures have a specific averaging scheme for these data (see programming example below for Campbell Scientific). Otherwise it is common practice to use a vector representation of wind and average its two horizontal components.

E.5   Sample Programs

In this section, sample programs for Campbell Scientific CR10 and CR10x data loggers are presented. Since the first printing of this manual Campbell Scientific has replaced the CR10 series with the CR1000, and a new programming scheme. Although the programs listed in this section cannot be used with the CR1000, the ideas and functions (such as sampling rates, averaging, maximum value) can be applied to new programs. The CR10(x) programs are presented as examples of how an automated weather station can be used to make a series of measurements and store data in two different time intervals. Weather station installers may have to alter these programs to fit their specific needs.

These sample programs are in a language specific to Campbell Scientific data loggers. Each command begins with a line number and is followed by a set of numbered parameters. Any line or section of text that begins with a semicolon is a comment and is not part of the command. These comments have been added to explain each programming operation.

Many avalanche operations in the United States use Campbell Scientific equipment. However, there are several companies that manufacture and distribute meteorological instruments in the United States. If your program uses equipment from a different manufacturer you can still use the methods outlined in these programs.

E.5.1   Sample Program – Basic Wind Site

```
;{CR10X}          ;Data logger type (CR10X)
;Station Information
;      Name
;      Number or ID
;      Elevation
;      History
;
;Program History
;      Date of implementation
;      Dates of revisions
;------------------------Begin Wiring Diagram
;Sensor #1: CS500 Relative Humidity and Temperature Probe
;CS500 Black  = 1H
;CS500 Brown  = 1L
;CS500 Red    = 12V
;CS500 Green  = G
;CS500 Clear  = G
;
;Sensor #2: 05103 Wind Monitor
;05103 SHIELD Clear = G
;05103 WSREF  Black = G
;05103 WDREF  Brown = AG
;05103 WDSIG  Red   = 2H
;05103 WDEXC  Green = E1
;05103 WSSIG  White = P1
;------------------------End Wiring Diagram
;
;------------------------Begin Program
*Table 1 Program
01: 5 Execution Interval (seconds)      ;Measurements are taken every 5 sec

1: Batt Voltage (P10)                   ;Sample Battery Voltage
1:1    Loc [ Battery ]

2: Internal Temperature (P17)           ;Sample the internal temperature
1:8    Loc [ IntTemp ]                  ;Note: This is recorded for diagnostic purposes and is
                                        ;not used in the program or output to the data file.

3: Volts (SE) (P1)                      ;Sample air temperature in degrees C.
1:1    Reps
2:25   2500 mV 60 Hz Rejection Range
3:1    SE Channel
4:2    Loc [ AIR_TEMP ]
5:.1   Mult                             ;See section F.4.2 for conversion to Fahrenheit.
6:-40  Offset

4: Volts (SE) (P1)                      ;Sample relative humidity in %
1:1    Reps
2:25   2500 mV 60 Hz Rejection Range
3:2    SE Channel
4:3    Loc [ RH ]
5:.1   Mult
6:0.0  Offset

;--------------------------Begin RH Error Check
;            Note: automated error checks can mask measurement errors and hinder
;            sensor diagnostics
5: IF (X<=>F) (P89)                     ;Check to see if the relative humidity is
1:3    X Loc [ RH ]                     ;greater than or equal to 100%. If it is, then perform
2:3    >=                               ;command number 6.
3:100  F
4:30   Then Do

6: Z=F (P30)                            ;Set the relative humidity to 100%.
1:100  F
2:0    Exponent of 10
3:3    Z Loc [ RH ]

7: End (P95)                            ;End of IF statement.
;--------------------------End of RH Error Check

8: Excite-Delay (SE) (P4)               ;Sample wind direction in degrees.
1:1    Reps
2:5    2500 mV Slow Range
3:3    SE Channel
4:1    Excite all reps w/Exchan 1
5:2    Delay (units 0.01 sec)
6:2500 mV Excitation
7:4    Loc [ WIND_DIR_ ]
8:.142 Mult
9:0    Offset

9: Pulse (P3)                           ;Sample wind speed in meters/second.
1:1    Reps
2:1    Pulse Input Channel
3:21   Low Level AC, Output Hz
4:5    Loc [ WIND_SPD ]
5:.0980 Mult                            ;For miles/hour use a multiplier of 0.2192. Always
6:0    Offset                           ;check instrument documentation for multiplier
                                        ;values.
;--------------------------Begin Data Output Section
;--------------------------15 Minute Data
10: If time is (P92)                    ;Write to output file every 15 min.
1:0    Minutes (Seconds --) into a
2:15   Interval (same units as above)
3:10   Set Output Flag High

11: Set Active Storage Area (P80)       ;Place 15 min data in storage area
1:2    Final Storage Area 2             ;number two.
```

2: 100   Array ID   ;Lines containing 15 min data will
                                                       ;begin with the array ID 100.

12: Real Time (P77)
1: 1110   Year, Day, Hour/Minute   ;Time format: 2003,1,0950
                                                       ;Year, Day of year, Hour min

13: Sample (P70)
1: 1   Reps
2: 1   Loc [Battery]   ;Output instantaneous battery
                                                       ;voltage.

14: Average (P71)
1: 1   Reps
2: 2   Loc [AIRTEMP]   ;Output 15 min average of air
                                                       ;temperature.

15: Average (P71)
1: 1   Reps
2: 3   Loc [RH]   ;Output 15 min average of relative
                                                       ;humidity.

16: Wind Vector (P69)
1: 1   Reps
2: 0   Samples per Sub-Interval
3: 1   S, 01 Polar
4: 5   Wind Speed/East Loc [WIND_SPD]
5: 4   Wind Direction/North Loc [WIND_DIR_]   ;Output 15 min average of wind
                                                       ;speed and vector averaged wind
                                                       ;direction.

17: Maximize (P73)
1: 1   Reps
2: 0   Value Only
3: 5   Loc [WIND_SPD]   ;Output maximum wind speed in
                                                       ;the 15 minute period.

18: Serial Out (P96)
1: 71   SM192/SM716/CSM1   ;Store data to storage module.

;-----------------------------------Hourly Data

19: If time is (P92)
1: 0   Minutes (Seconds --) into a
2: 60   Interval (same units as above)
3: 10   Set Output Flag High   ;Write to output file every hour.

20: Set Active Storage Area (P80)
1: 1   Final Storage Area 1
21: 101   Array ID   ;Place hourly data in storage area
                                                       ;number one.
                                                       ;Lines containing 15 min data will
                                                       ;begin with the array ID 100.

22: Real Time (P77)
1: 1110   Year, Day, Hour/Minute   ;Time format: 2003,1,0950
                                                       ;Year, Day of year, hour min

13: Sample (P70)
1: 1   Reps
2: 1   Loc [Battery]   ;Output instantaneous battery
                                                       ;voltage.

23: Average (P71)
1: 1   Reps
2: 2   Loc [AIRTEMP]   ;Output hourly average of air temperature

24: Average (P71)
1: 1   Reps
2: 3   Loc [RH]   ;Output hourly average of relative
                                                       ;humidity.

25: Wind Vector (P69)
1: 1   Reps
2: 0   Samples per Sub-Interval
3: 1   S, 01 Polar
4: 5   Wind Speed/East Loc [WIND_SPD]
5: 4   Wind Direction/North Loc [WIND_DIR_]   ;Output hourly average of wind
                                                       ;speed and vector averaged wind
                                                       ;direction.

26: Maximize (P73)
1: 1   Reps
2: 0   Value Only
3: 5   Loc [WIND_SPD]   ;Output maximum wind speed in
                                                       ;the 1 hour period.

27: Serial Out (P96)
1: 71   SM192/SM716/CSM1   ;Store data to storage module.

End Program

Program Output
Final Storage Location 1
101,2003,1,0800,12.42,5.24,68.45,8.34,270,15.93
101,2003,1,0900,12.40,7.45,60.34,4.72,275,8.30
Final Storage Location 2
100,2003,1,0800,12.42,5.69,68.23,8.46,270,14.35
100,2003,1,0815,12.41,5.94,66.57,7.20,272,12.30

E.5.2 Sample Program – Basic Precipitation Site

```
;{CR10X}
;Station Information
;      Name
;      Number or ID
;      Elevation
;      History
;
;Program History
;      Date of implementation
;      Dates of revisions
;                                              -----Begin Wiring Diagram

;Sensor #1 Judd Communication Depth Sensor, Interval
;Clear = G
;Black = G
;Red   = 12V
;Green = C1
;White = 1H
;Brown = G
;
;Sensor #2 Judd Communication Depth Sensor, Total
;Clear = G
;Black = G
;Red   = 12V
;Green = C1
;White = 1L
;Brown = G
;
;Sensor #3: ETI Precipitation Gauge
;Red   = 12V
;Black = G
;Green = P2
;
;                                            -----End Wiring Diagram

*Table 1 Program
  01: 5      Execution Interval (seconds)    ;Measurements are taken every 5 seconds.

1: Batt Voltage (P10)                        ;Sample battery voltage.
1: 1    Loc [ Battery ]

2: Pulse (P3)                                ;Sample precipitation from ETI gauge.
1: 1    Reps
2: 2    Pulse Input Channel
3: 2    Switch Closure
4: 8    Loc [ PRECIP  ]
5: .01  Mult
6: 0    Offset

;                                            -----Begin Depth Sensor Call
;                                            -----Begin Depth Sensor Status Check
3: If time is (P92)                          ;Perform command every 15 minutes.
1: 0     Minutes (Seconds --) into a
2: 15    Interval (same units as above)
3: 30    Then Do

4: If Flag/Port (P91)                        ;If the depth sensor is on, turn it off.
1: 11    Do if Flag 1 is High
2: 21    Set Flag 1 Low

5: End (P95)                                  ;            -----End Depth Sensor Status Check
;
6: If Flag/Port (P91)                        ;This command allows for an instantaneous
1: 11    Do if Flag 1 is High                ;measurement of the snow depth from a PC
2: 1     Call Subroutine 1                   ;that is connected to the data logger (press F1).

7: If time is (P92)                          ;Call subroutine that measures snow depth
1: 0     Minutes (Seconds --) into a
2: 15    Interval (same units as above)
3: 1     Call Subroutine 1

;                                            -----Begin Data Output Section
;                                            -----15 Minute Data
8: If time is (P92)                          ;Specify 15 minute output interval.
1: 0     Minutes (Seconds --) into a
2: 15    Interval (same units as above)
3: 10    Set Output Flag High

9: Set Active Storage Area (P80)             ;Place 15 min data in storage area number two.
1: 2     Final Storage Area 2
2: 100   Array ID                            ;Lines containing 15 min data will begin with the
                                             ;array ID 100.

10: Real Time (P77)                          ;Time format: 2003,1,0950
1: 1110  Year, Day, Hour/Minute              ;Year, Day of year, hour min

11: Sample (P70)                             ;Output instantaneous battery voltage
1: 1     Reps
2: 1     Loc [ Battery ]

12: Sample (P70)                             ;Output instantaneous air temperature from
1: 1     Reps                                ;the interval depth sensor.
2: 2     Loc [ DSTemp1 ]
```

Snow, Weather, and Avalanches

```
13: Sample (P70)                         ;Output instantaneous snow depth from the
 1: 1      Reps                          ;interval depth sensor.
 2: 3      Loc [ IntSnow ]

14: Sample (P70)                         ;Output instantaneous snow depth from the
 1: 1      Reps                          ;total snow depth sensor.
 2: 4      Loc [ TotalSnow ]

15: Totalize (P72)                       ;Output the total liquid precipitation from
 1: 1      Reps                          ;the ETI gauge.
 2: 8      Loc [ PRECIP ]

16: Serial Out (P96)                     ;Store data to storage module.
 1: 71     SM192/SM716/CSM1

;
;-------------------------------- Hourly Data

17: If time is (P92)                     ;Specify 60 minute output interval.
 1: 0      Minutes (Seconds --) into a
 2: 60     Interval (same units as above)
 3: 10     Set Output Flag High

18: Set Active Storage Area (P80)        ;Lines containing 15 min data will
21: 101    Array ID                      ;begin with the array ID 100.

19: Real Time (P77)                      ;Time format: 2003,1,0950
 1: 1110   Year, Day, Hour/Minute        ;Year, Day of year, hour min

20: Sample (P70)                         ;Output instantaneous battery voltage.
 1: 1      Reps
 2: 1      Loc [ Battery ]

21: Sample (P70)                         ;Output instantaneous air temperature
 1: 1      Reps                          ;from the interval snow depth sensor.
 2: 2      Loc [ DSTemp1 ]

22: Sample (P70)                         ;Output instantaneous snow depth from the
 1: 1      Reps                          ;interval snow depth sensor.
 2: 3      Loc [ IntSnow ]

23: Sample (P70)                         ;Output instantaneous snow depth from the
 1: 1      Reps                          ;total snow depth sensor.
 2: 4      Loc [ TotalSnow ]

24: Totalize (P72)                       ;Output the total liquid precipitation from
 1: 1      Reps                          ;the ETI gauge.
 2: 8      Loc [ PRECIP ]

25: Serial Out (P96)                     ;Store data to storage module.
 1: 71     SM192/SM716/CSM1

*Table 3 Subroutines

 1: Beginning of Subroutine (P85)        ;Begin subroutine and label it number 1.
 1: 1      Subroutine 1

;-------------------------------- Begin Snow Depth Subroutine

 2: Do (P86)                             ;Turn on both snow depth sensors
 1: 41     Set Port 1 High               ;(see wiring diagram).

 3: Excitation with Delay (P22)          ;Wait 0.6 seconds for the sensor to
 1: 1      Ex Channel                    ;measure the air temperature
 2: 60     Delay W/Ex (units = 0.01 sec)
 3: 0      Delay After Ex (units = 0.01 sec)
 4: 0      mV Excitation

 4: Excite-Delay (SE) (P4)               ;Sample air temperature in degrees C
 1: 1      Reps                          ;from the interval snow depth sensor.
 2: 5      2500 mV Slow Range
 3: 1      SE Channel
 4: 1      Excite all reps w/Exchan 1
 5: 0      Delay (units 0.01 sec)
 6: 0      mV Excitation
 7: 2      Loc [ DSTemp1 ]
 8: .2     Mult
 9: -273   Offset

 5: Excite-Delay (SE) (P4)               ;Sample air temperature in degrees C
 1: 1      Reps                          ;from the total snow depth sensor.
 2: 5      ñ 2500 mV Slow Range
 3: 2      SE Channel
 4: 1      Excite all reps w/Exchan 1
 5: 0      Delay (units 0.01 sec)
 6: 0      mV Excitation
 7: 7      Loc [ DSTemp2 ]
 8: .2     Mult
 9: -273   Offset

 6: Excitation with Delay (P22)          ;Wait 1.8 seconds for the sensor to make
 1: 1      Ex Channel                    ;10 measurements and perform air
 2: 180    Delay W/Ex (units = 0.01 sec) ;temperature compensation.
 3: 0      Delay After Ex (units = 0.01 sec)
 4: 0      mV Excitation

 7: Excite-Delay (SE) (P4)               ;Sample interval snow depth in
 1: 1      Reps                          ;centimeters.
 2: 5      2500 mV Slow Range
```

114

Appendix E: Automated Weather Stations

```
3: 1     SE Channel
4: 1     Excite all reps w/Exchan 1
5: 0     Delay (units 0.01 sec)
6: 0     mV Excitation
7: 3     Loc [ IntSnow ]
8: -0.5  Mult
9: 100   Offset              ;This value outputs snow depth in centimeters
                             ;Use -0.19685 for inches.
                             ;This number is the distance between the sensor
                             ;and the ground surface in centimeters.

8: Excite-Delay (SE) (P4)     ;Sample total snow depth in centimeters.
1: 1     Reps
2: 5     2500 mV Slow Range
3: 2     SE Channel
4: 1     Excite all reps w/Exchan 1
5: 0     Delay (units 0.01 sec)
6: 0     mV Excitation
7: 4     Loc [ TotalSnow ]
8: -0.5  Mult
9: 1000  Offset              ;This value outputs snow depth in centimeters
                             ;Use -0.19685 for inches.
                             ;This number is the distance between the sensor
                             ;and the ground surface in centimeters.

9: Do (P86)
1: 51    Set Port 1 Low       ;Turn off snow depth sensors.

10: End (P95)                  ;End of snow depth subroutine

End Program                    ;End of program

Program Output
Final Storage Location 1
    101,2003,1,0800,12.42,5.24,8.30,140.34,0.59
    101,2003,1,0900,12.40,7.45,9.53,141.83,0.63
Final Storage Location 2
    100,2003,1,0800,12.42,5.26,8.30,140.36,0.58
    100,2003,1,0815,12.41,5.94,8.34,140.7,0.59
```

E.5.2   Sample Program – Temperature Conversion

The air temperature measurements in the program examples are output in degrees kelvin. Within the sampling commands the temperatures are converted from degrees kelvin to degrees Celsius. The commands listed below can be added to any Campbell Scientific program to convert a temperature in degrees Celsius to degrees Fahrenheit.

```
#: Z=X*F (P37)
1: 2     X Loc [ AIRTEMPF ]     ;Multiply the air temperature in degrees
2: 1.8   F                      ;C by 1.8 and store it in the same location.
3: 2     Z Loc [ AIRTEMPF ]

#: Z=X+F (P34)
1: 2     X Loc [ AIRTEMPF ]     ;Add 32 to the new value to complete
2: 32    F                      ;the conversion. The temperature
3: 2     Z Loc [ AIRTEMPF ]     ;in degrees F is stored in the same
                                ;location.
```

Snow, Weather, and Avalanches

Appendix F
ICSI Classification for Seasonal Snow on the Ground

Basic classification	Morphological classification				Additional information on physical processes and strength		
	Subclass	Shape	Code	Place of formation	Physical process	Dependence on most important parameters	Common effect on strength
Precipitation Particles +			**PP**				
	Columns □	Prismatic crystal, solid or hollow	PPco	Cloud; temperature inversion layer (clear sky)	Growth from water vapour at −3 to −8 °C and below−30 °C		
	Needles ↕	Needle-like, approximately cylindrical	PPnd	Cloud	Growth from water vapour at high supersaturation at −3 to −5 °C and below −60 °C		
	Plates ⬡	Plate-like, mostly hexagonal	PPpl	Cloud; temperature inversion layer (clear sky)	Growth from water vapour at 0 to −3 °C and −8 to −70 °C		
	Stellars, Dendrites ✱	Six-fold star-like, planar or spatial	PPsd	Cloud; temperature inversion layer (clear sky)	Growth from water vapour at high supersaturation at 0 to −3 °C and at −12 to −16 °C		
	Irregular crystals	Clusters of very small crystals	PPir	Cloud	Polycrystals growing in varying environmental conditions		
	Graupel	Heavily rimed particles, spherical, conical, hexagonal, or irregular in shape	PPgp	Cloud	Heavy riming of particles by accretion of supercooled water droplets Size: ≤ 5 mm		
	Hail ◀	Laminar internal structure, translucent or milky glazed surface	PPhl	Cloud	Growth by accretion of supercooled water Size: > 5 mm		
	Ice pellets	Transparent, mostly small spheroids	PPip	Cloud	Freezing of raindrops or refreezing of largely melted snow crystals or snowflakes (sleet) Graupel or snow pellets encased in thin ice layer (small hail) Size: both ≤ 5 mm		
	Rime	Irregular deposits or longer cones and needles pointing into the wind	PPrm	Onto surface as well as on freely exposed objects	Accretion of small, supercooled fog droplets frozen in place. Thin breakable crust forms on snow surface if process continues long enough	Increase with fog density and exposure to wind	

	Morphological classification				Additional information on physical processes and strength		
Basic classification	Subclass	Shape	Code	Place of formation	Physical process	Dependence on most important parameters	Common effect on strength
Machine Made snow			**MM**				
◎	Round polycrystalline particles	Small spherical particles, often showing protrusions, a result of the freezing process; may be partially hollow	MMrp	Atmosphere, near surface	Machined snow, i.e., freezing of very small water droplets from the surface inward	Liquid water content depends mainly on air temperature and humidity but also on snow density and grain size	In dry conditions, quick sintering results in rapid strength increase
✍	Crushed ice particles	Ice plates, shard-like	MMci	Ice generators	Machined ice, i.e., production of flake ice, subsequent crushing, and pneumatic distribution	All weather safe	
Decomposing and Fragmented precipitation particles			**DF**				
/	Partly decomposed precipitation particles	Characteristic shapes of precipitation particles still recognizable; often partly rounded.	DFdc	Within the snowpack; recently deposited snow near the surface, usually dry	Decrease of surface area to reduce surface free energy; also fragmentation due to light winds lead to initial break up	Speed of decomposition decreases with decreasing snow temperatures and decreasing temperature gradients	Regains cohesion by sintering after initial strength decreased due to decomposition
/	Wind-broken precipitation particles	Shards or fragments of precipitation particles	DFbk	Surface layer, mostly recently deposited snow	Saltation particles are fragmented and packed by wind, often closely; fragmentation often followed by rounding	Fragmentation and packing by wind, increase with wind speed	Quick sintering results in rapid strength increase

Rounded Grains

Basic classification	Morphological classification			Additional information on physical processes and strength			
	Subclass	Shape	Code	Place of formation	Physical process	Dependence on most important parameters	Common effect on strength
			RG				
	Small rounded particles	Rounded, usually elongated particles of size < 0.25 mm; highly sintered	RGsr	Within the snowpack; dry snow	Decrease of specific surface area by slow decrease of number of grains and increase of mean grain diameter. Small equilibrium growth form	Growth rate increases with increasing temperature; growth slower in high density snow with smaller pores	Strength due to sintering of the snow grains [1]. Strength increases with time, settlement and decreasing grain size
	Large rounded particles	Rounded, usually elongated particles of size ≥ 0.25 mm; well sintered	RGlr	Within the snowpack; dry snow	Grain-to-grain vapour diffusion due to low temperature gradients, i.e., mean excess vapour density remains below critical value for kinetic growth. Large equilibrium growth form	Same as above	Same as above
	Wind packed	Small, broken or abraded, closely-packed particles; well sintered	RGwp	Surface layer; dry snow	Packing and fragmentation of wind transported snow particles that round off by interaction with each other in the saltation layer. Evolves into either a hard but usually breakable wind crust or a thicker wind slab. (see notes)	Hardness increases with wind speed, decreasing particle size and moderate temperature	High number of contact points and small size causes rapid strength increase through sintering
	Faceted rounded particles	Rounded, usually elongated particles with developing facets	RGxf	Within the snowpack; dry snow	Growth regime changes if mean excess vapour density is larger than critical value for kinetic growth. Accordingly, this transitional form develops facets as temperature gradient increases	Grains are changing in response to an increasing temperature gradient	Reduction in number of bonds may decrease strength

Morphological classification / Additional information on physical processes and strength

Basic classification	Subclass	Shape	Code	Place of formation	Physical process	Dependence on most important parameters	Common effect on strength
Faceted Crystals ☐			FC		Grain-to-grain vapour diffusion driven by large enough temperature gradient, i.e., excess vapour density is above critical value for kinetic growth	Growth rate increases with temperature, increasing temperature gradient, and decreasing density; may not grow to larger grains in high density snow because of small pores	Strength decreases with increasing growth rate and grain size
	Solid faceted particles ☐	Solid faceted crystals; usually hexagonal prisms	FCso	Within the snowpack; dry snow	Solid kinetic growth form, i.e., a solid crystal with sharp edges and corners as well as glassy, smooth faces		
	Near surface faceted particles ☑	Faceted crystals in surface layer	FCsf	Within the snowpack but right beneath the surface; dry snow	May develop directly from Precipitation Particles (PP) or Decomposing and Fragmented particles (DFdc) due to large, near-surface temperature gradients [1]	Temperature gradient may periodically change sign but remains at a high absolute value	Low strength snow
	Rounding faceted particles ⊟	Faceted crystals with rounding facets and corners	FCxr	Within the snowpack; dry snow	Solid kinetic growth form (see FCso above) at early stage of development. Trend to a transitional form reducing its specific surface area; corners and edges of the crystals are rounding off	Grains are rounding off in response to a decreasing temperature gradient	

Morphological classification

Additional information on physical processes and strength

Basic classification	Subclass	Shape	Code	Place of formation	Physical process	Dependence on most important parameters	Common effect on strength
Depth Hoar ∧			**DH**		Grain-to-grain vapour diffusion driven by large temperature gradient, i.e., excess vapour density is well above critical value for kinetic growth.		
	Hollow cups ∧	Striated, hollow skeleton type crystals; usually cup-shaped	DHcp	Within the snowpack; dry snow	Formation of hollow or partly solid cup-shaped kinetic growth crystals [1]	See FCso.	Usually fragile but strength increases with density
	Hollow prisms ⊓	Prismatic, hollow skeleton type crystals with glassy faces but few striations	DHpr	Within the snowpack; dry snow	Snow has completely recrystallized; high temperature gradient in low density snow, most often prolonged [2]	High recrystallization rate for long period and low density snow facilitates formation	May be very poorly bonded
	Chains of depth hoar ∧	Hollow skeleton type crystals arranged in chains	DHch	Within the snowpack; dry snow	Snow has completely recrystallized; inter-granular arrangement in chains; most of the lateral bonds between columns have disappeared during crystal growth	High recrystallization rate for long period and low density snow facilitates formation	Very fragile snow
	Large striated crystals A	Large, heavily striated crystals; either solid or skeleton type	DHla	Within the snowpack; dry snow	Evolves from earlier stages described above; some bonding occurs as new crystals are initiated [2]	Longer time required than for any other snow crystal; long periods of large temperature gradient in low density snow are needed	Regains strength
	Rounding depth hoar ∧	Hollow skeleton type crystals with rounding of sharp edges, corners, and striations	DHxr	Within the snowpack; dry snow	Trend to a form reducing its specific surface area; corners and edges of the crystals are rounding off; faces may loose their relief, i.e., striations and steps disappear slowly. This process effects all subclasses of depth hoar	Grains are rounding off in response to a decreasing temperature gradient	May regain strength

Surface Hoar — SH

Basic classification	Morphological classification			Additional information on physical processes and strength			
	Subclass	Shape	Code	Place of formation	Physical process	Dependence on most important parameters	Common effect on strength
Surface Hoar	Surface hoar crystals	Striated, usually flat crystals; sometimes needle-like	SHsu	Usually on cold snow surface of crystals at the snow surface; sometimes on freely exposed objects above the surface (see notes)	Rapid kinetic growth of crystals at the snow surface by rapid transfer of water vapour from the atmosphere toward the snow surface; snow surface cooled to below ambient temperature by radiative cooling	Both increased cooling of the snow surface below air temperature as well as increasing relative humidity of the air cause growth rate to increase. In high water vapour gradient fields, e.g., near creeks, large feathery crystals may develop	Fragile, extremely low shear strength; strength may remain low for extended periods when buried in cold dry snow
	Cavity or crevasse hoar	Striated, planar or large hollow skeleton type crystals grown in cavities; orientation often random	SHcv	Cavity hoar is found in large voids in the snow, e.g., in the vicinity of tree trunks, buried bushes [1]. Crevasse hoar is found in any large cooled space such as crevasses, cold storage rooms, boreholes, etc.	kinetic growth of crystals forming anywhere where a cavity, i.e., a large cooled space, is formed or present in which water vapour can be deposited under calm, still conditions [2]		
	Rounding surface hoar	Surface hoar crystal with rounding of sharp edges, corners and striations	SHxr	Within the snowpack; dry snow	Trend to a form reducing its specific surface area; corners and edges of the crystals are rounding off; faces may loose their relief, i.e., striations and steps disappear slowly	Grains are rounding off in response to a decreasing temperature gradient	May regain strength

Morphological classification

Additional information on physical processes and strength

Basic classification	Subclass	Shape	Code	Place of formation	Physical process	Dependence on most important parameters	Common effect on strength
Melt Forms O			MF				
	Clustered rounded grains	Clustered rounded crystals held by large ice-to-ice bonds; water in internal veins among three crystals or two grain boundaries	MFcl	At the surface or within the snowpack; wet snow	Wet snow at low water content (pendular regime), i.e., holding free liquid water; clusters form to minimize surface free energy	Meltwater can drain; too much water leads to MFsl; first freezing leads to MFpc	Ice-to-ice bonds give strength
	Rounded polycrystals	Individual crystals are frozen into a solid polycrystalline particle, either wet or refrozen	MFpc	At the surface or within the snowpack	Melt-freeze cycles form polycrystals when water in veins freezes; either wet at low water content (pendular regime) or refrozen	Particle size increases with number of melt-freeze cycles; radiation penetration may restore MFcl; excess water leads to MFsl	High strength in the frozen state; lower strength in the wet state; strength increases with number of melt-freeze cycles
	Slush	Separated rounded particles completely immersed in water	MFsl	Water saturated, soaked snow; found within the snowpack, on land or ice surfaces, but also as a viscous floating mass in water after heavy snowfall.	Wet snow at high liquid water content (funicular regime); poorly bonded, fully rounded single crystals – and polycrystals – form as ice and water are in thermodynamic equilibrium	Water drainage blocked by capillary barrier, impermeable layer or ground; high energy input to the snowpack by solar radiation, high air temperature or water input (rain)	Little strength due to decaying bonds
	Melt-freeze crust	Crust of recognizable melt-freeze polycrystals	MFcr	At the surface	Crust of melt-freeze polycrystals from a surface layer of wet snow that refroze after having been wetted by melt or rainfall; found either wet or refrozen	Particle size and density increases with number of melt-freeze cycles	Strength increases with number of melt-freeze cycles

Ice Formations

Basic classification	Morphological classification				Additional information on physical processes and strength		
	Subclass	Shape	Code	Place of formation	Physical process	Dependence on most important parameters	Common effect on strength
Ice Formations ■	Ice layer ■	Horizontal ice layer	IFil	Within the snowpack	Rain or meltwater from the surface percolates into cold snow where it refreezes along layer-parallel capillary barriers by heat conduction into surrounding subfreezing snow, i.e., snow at T < 0 °C; ice layers usually retain some degree of permeability	Depends on timing of percolating water and cycles of melting and refreezing; more likely to occur if a stratification of fine over coarse-grained layers exists	Ice layers are strong but strength decays once snow is completely wetted
	Ice column ■	Vertical ice body	IFic	Within snowpack layers	Draining water within flow fingers freezes by heat conduction into surrounding subfreezing snow, i.e., snow at T < 0 °C	Flow fingers more likely to occur if snow is highly stratified; freezing enhanced if snow is very cold	
	Basal ice □	Basal ice layer	IFbi	Base of snowpack	Melt water ponds above substrate and freezes by heat conduction into cold substrate	Formation enhanced if substrate is impermeable and very cold, e.g., permafrost	Weak slush layer may form on top
	Rain crust =	Thin, transparent glaze or clear film of ice on the surface	IFrc	At the surface	Results from freezing rain on snow; forms a thin surface glaze	Droplets have to be supercooled but coalesce before freezing	Thin breakable crust
	Sun crust, Firnspiegel —	Thin, transparent and shiny glaze or clear film of ice on the surface	IFsc	At the surface	Melt water from a surface snow layer refreezes at the surface due to radiative cooling; decreasing shortwave absorption in the forming glaze enhances greenhouse effect in the underlying snow; additional water vapour may condense below the glaze [1]	Builds during clear weather, air temperatures below freezing and strong solar radiation; not to be confused with melt-freeze crust MFcr	Thin breakable crust

Appendix F: ICSI International Classification for Seasonal Snow on the Ground

Rounded Polycrystals and Melt-Freeze Crust

To distinguish between rounded polycrystals (Class 6b or WGmf) and a melt-freeze crust (Class 9e or CRmfc), consider the structural units. If a crust layer is broken apart, the result is lumps of variable size since the crust (of indeterminate length and width) is the structural unit. If a portion of a layer of frozen rounded polycrystals is broken apart, the result is quite consistently sized particles (the individual polycrystals).

When formed by freezing rain, rain crusts (Class 9b or CRrc) are often thin, fragile transparent layers that form on the surface. Rain more commonly forms melt-freeze crust (Class 9e or CRmfc), which can vary from thin (several mm to 1 cm) to thick (>5 cm) layers.

Sun crusts (Class 9d or CRsc) are thin, fragile transparent layers that form on the surface. More commonly, direct sun causes a melting of the snow that results in a melt-freeze crust (Class 9e or CRmfc).

Wind crusts (Class 9c or CRwc) are thin irregular layers of small, broken or abraded, closely packed and well-sintered particles (usually found on windward slopes). The particles in these layers may be similar in appearance to those in wind slabs (usually found on lee slopes); however, some authors report that particle size is more variable in wind crusts than wind slabs.

Surface Hoar

Sub-classes listed in Table F.1 can be used to record different types of surface hoar (7a).

Table F.1 Sub-classes of surface hoar (based on Jamieson and Schweizer, 2000)

Sub-class	Description	Formation Temperature
i. Needle	Primarily one dimensional, sometimes spike- or sheath-like	Below -21°C
ii. Plate	Two-dimensional sector plate; usually wedge shaped and narrow at base. Usually striated when formed; however, the striations may disappear while buried in the snowpack	-10°C to -21°C
iii. Dendrite	Two-dimensional form with numerous branches; often feather-like in appearance; narrow at base	-10°C to -21°C
iv. Cup or scrolls	Three-dimensional; these form with narrow base on surface of the snowpack; once separated from the snowpack, these forms can be indistinguishable from depth hoar-cup crystals	
v. Composite forms	Combinations of shapes associated with subclasses i to iv	

Refer to Colbeck and others (1990) for further explanation of shapes, place of formation, classifications, physical processes and common effects on strength. The document is online at: http://www.crrel.usace.army.mil/techpub/CRREL_Reports/html_files/Cat_A.html.

Snow, Weather, and Avalanches

Appendix G
Avalanche Danger, Hazard, and Snow Stability Scales

G.1 Introduction

There are many ways to communicate the current avalanche conditions. Categorical scales of avalanche danger, avalanche hazard, and snow stability can improve communication amongst forecasts and between forecasters and customers. Forecasting operation managers should select an appropriate scale based on the definitions that follow. The scales presented in this appendix are examples of commonly used communication methods.

G.2 Definitions

Stability

The chance that avalanches *do not* initiate. Stability is analyzed in space and time relative to a given triggering level or load.

Exposure— An element or resource (person, vehicle, structure, etc…) that is subject to the impact of a specific natural hazard.

Hazard, Avalanche—The potential for an avalanche(s) to cause damage to something of value. It is a combination of the likelihood of triggering and the destructive size of the avalanche(s). It implies the potential to affect people, facilities or things of value, but does not incorporate vulnerability or exposure to avalanches. Avalanche danger and hazard are synonymous and are commonly expressed using relative terms such as high, moderate and low.

Risk— The chance of something happening that will have an impact on an element (person, vehicle, structure, etc…). A risk is often specified in terms of an event or circumstance and the consequences that may follow. Risk is evaluated in terms of a combination of the consequences of an event and their likelihood.

Vulnerability— The degree to which an exposed element (person, vehicle, structure, etc…) is susceptible the impact of a specific natural hazard.

Figure G.1 Vegetation damage from a large avalanche (photograph by John Stimberis).

G.3 General Guidelines for the use of Avalanche Conditions Scales

Avalanche conditions within a forecast area can be separated based on terrain or snowpack characteristics.

Specify the area based on:

- Elevations
    - Numerical range
    - Geographic feature (i.e. Alpine, Treeline, Below Treeline)
- Aspect
- Slope angle
- Specific conditions such as wind loaded slopes or depth of new snow
- Spatial extent (localized or widespread)
- Time of day
    Note: Timberline (treeline) describes a transition area between closed forest and the open treeless areas above.

Where practical give the expected stability trend for the next 12 to 24 hours. Use the terms: improving, steady, and decreasing stability to describe the trend.

Specify a confidence level in the ratings when appropriate; describe sources of uncertainty in forecast. Note the level of the unstable layer in the snowpack (i.e. near surface, mid level, deep).

Observers may qualify the rating based on:

- Topography (aspect, slope angle, etc.)
- Spatial extent (localized or widespread)
- Time of day

Figure G.2 Widespread avalanche activity within a single drainage (photograph by Craig Sterbenz).

Appendix G: Avalanche Danger, Hazard, and Snow Stability Scales

G.4   Snow Stability Scale

Stability refers to the chance that avalanches will *not* initiate, and does *not* predict the size or potential consequences of expected avalanches. Avalanche hazard and risk evaluation includes consideration of these factors. "It is possible for highly unstable snow to exist with no hazard if people or facilities are not threatened" (McClung and Schaerer, 1993).

> *Note: Statements about avalanche activity take precedence over results of stability tests.*

> *For regional and larger forecast areas, isolated natural avalanches may occur even when stability for the area as a whole is good.*

Table G.1 Snow Stability Rating System

Stability		Expected Avalanche Activity		
Stability Rating	**Comment on Snow Stability**	**Natural Avalanches** (*excluding* avalanches triggered by icefall, cornice fall, or rock fall)	**Triggered Avalanches** (*including* avalanches triggered by human action, icefall, cornice fall, rock fall or wildlife)	**Expected Results of Stability Tests**
Very Good (VG)	Snowpack is stable	No natural avalanches expected	Avalanches may be triggered by very heavy loads such as large cornice falls or loads in isolated terrain features	Generally little or no result
Good (G)	Snowpack is mostly stable	No natural avalanches expected	Avalanches may be triggered by heavy loads in isolated terrain features	Generally moderate to hard results
Fair (F)	Snowpack stability varies considerably with terrain, often resulting in locally unstable areas	Isolated natural avalanches on specific terrain features	Avalanches may be triggered by light loads in areas with specific terrain features or certain snowpack characteristics	Generally easy to moderate results
Poor (P)	Snowpack is mostly unstable	Natural avalanches in areas with specific terrain features or certain snowpack characteristics	Avalanches may be triggered by light loads in many areas with sufficiently steep slopes	Generally easy results
Very Poor (VP)	Snowpack is very unstable	Widespread natural avalanches	Widespread triggering of avalanches by light loads	Generally very easy to easy results

Definitions / Examples

- Natural avalanches: Avalanches triggered by weather events such as snowfall, rain, wind, temperature changes, etc.
- Heavy load: A cornice fall, a compact group of people, a snowmobile or explosives.
- Light load: A single person, or a small cornice fall.
- Isolated terrain features: Extreme terrain; steep convex rolls; localized dispersed areas (pockets) without readily specifiable characteristics.
- Specific terrain features: Lee slopes, sun-exposed aspects.
- Certain snowpack characteristics: Shallow snowpack with faceted grains, persistent weaknesses, identified weaknesses.

G.5   Avalanche Danger Scale

The Avalanche Danger presented in this section is used by regional avalanche forecast centers in the United States. The scale was designed to facilitate communication between forecasters and the public. The categories represent the probability of avalanche activity and recommend travel precautions.

Note: The current North American Avalanche Danger Scale presented below is currently being revised. A new scale for public avalanche bulletins will likely be published in 2010.

Table G.2 The United States Avalanche Danger Scale (after Dennis and Moore, 1996).

Danger Level (color) ...What...	Avalanche Probability and Avalanche Trigger ...Why...	Degree and Distribution of Avalanche Danger ...Where...	Recommended Action in the Backcountry ...What to do...
LOW (green)	Natural avalanches very unlikely. Human triggered avalanches <u>unlikely</u>.	Generally stable snow. Isolated areas of instability.	Travel is generally safe. Normal caution advised.
MODERATE (yellow)	Natural avalanches unlikely. Human triggered avalanches <u>possible</u>.	Unstable slabs <u>possible</u> on steep terrain.	Use caution in steep terrain on certain aspects (defined in accompanying statement).
CONSIDERABLE (orange)	Natural avalanches possible. Human triggered avalanches <u>probable</u>.	Unstable slabs <u>probable</u> on steep terrain.	Be increasingly cautious in steep terrain.
HIGH (red)	Natural and human triggered avalanches <u>likely</u>.	Unstable slabs <u>likely</u> on a variety of aspects and slope angles.	Travel in avalanche terrain is not recommended. Safest travel on windward ridges of lower angle slopes without steeper terrain above.
EXTREME (red with black border)	Widespread natural or human triggered avalanches <u>certain.</u>	Extremely unstable slabs <u>certain</u> on most aspects and slope angles. Large and destructive avalanches possible.	Travel in avalanche terrain should be avoided and travel confined to low angle terrain well away from avalanche path run-outs.

Appendix G: Avalanche Danger, Hazard, and Snow Stability Scales

G.6 Avalanche Hazard Scale

Avalanche hazard scales can be used when forecasting the threat of avalanches to structures and transportation arteries. The scale should be tailored for each individual operation. Table G.3 contains a scale used by the Colorado Avalanche Information Center/Colorado Department of Transportation. This scale is presented as an example of an operational avalanche hazard scale.

Note: Arrows may be used to indicate the trend in avalanche hazard. Avalanche control operations may be recommended at any condition rating.

Table G.3 Avalanche Hazard Scale

Hazard Level	Description	Operational Impact
None	Insufficient snow for avalanches to reach the highway.	Normal highway operations.
Low	Mostly stable snow. Natural avalanches are unlikely to affect the highway. Small triggered and natural avalanches are possible.	Normal highway operations.
Moderate	Areas of unstable snow. Natural and triggered avalanches possible. A moderate amount of snow on the highway is possible.	Normal highway operations continue with caution. Explosive mitigation may be necessary.
High	Mostly unstable snow. Natural and triggered avalanches across the highway are likely. A moderate to large amount of snow on the highway is possible.	Highway closure may be necessary. Explosive mitigation will be required. Maintenance and emergency traffic may continue prior to avalanche control if hazard and need warrants.
Extreme	Widespread unstable snow. Natural and triggered avalanches certain. A large amount of snow on the highway is likely.	Highway closure necessary until explosive mitigation completed.

Figure G.3 An explosive triggered avalanche strikes Colorado Highway 160 near Wolf Creek Pass (photograph by Mark Mueller).

Snow, Weather, and Avalanches

Appendix H
Reporting Avalanche Involvements

H.1   Objective
The objective of reporting avalanche accidents and damage is to collect data about the extent of avalanche hazards in the United States. Summaries of the reports will draw attention to avalanche problems and assist in the development of risk reduction measures.

H.2   Reporting Forms
Two different reports are available for recording avalanche accidents and damage. Any person who wishes to report an avalanche incident or accident can use these reports.

The short form is a brief summary of an avalanche incident or accident. This form should be submitted every time people are involved in an avalanche, property is damaged or a significant natural event occurs.

The long form is a detailed report that can be used as a template for an accident investigation. This report should be completed when an avalanche causes a fatality, serious injury, or property damage in excess of $5,000, or when the incident has a high educational value. It may be useful as a checklist when operations wish to describe an accident and rescue work in greater detail.

H.3   Filing of Reports
Completed short reports should be returned as quickly as possible to the nearest avalanche center. A copy should also be sent to the Colorado Avalanche Information Center, which serves as a central recording hub for avalanche accident information.

> Colorado Avalanche Information Center
> 325 Broadway #WS1
> Boulder, CO 80305
> caic@qwestoffice.net
> Voice: (303)499-9650
> Fax: (303) 499-9618
> www.colorado.gov/avalanche

Reports will be used to identify trends in avalanche accidents, used for educational purposes, and to maintain long-term data sets. The reporter's and victim's names and contact information should be recorded. Requests for anonymity will be noted and respected whenever possible.

H.4   Completing the Short Form
H.4.1   Date and Time
Fill in the date and time of the avalanche occurrence.

H.4.2   Location
Give the mountain range, valley and feature where the avalanche occurred. Include as much information as possible including county name, ski area name, highway name, avalanche path and GPS coordinates.

H.4.3   Group and Activity Description
Record the primary purpose of the group when the avalanche occurred. Enter the number of people engaged in each listed activity. If the activity is not listed write it in (i.e. mountain climbing, snowshoeing, traveling on a road). Note if the group was ascending, descending, etc.

H.4.4   People Caught in the Avalanche
Enter the number of people that were involved in the avalanche and the number injured or killed. Of those involved, give the number that were not caught or buried; the number *caught;* the number that were *partially buried–not critical*; the number that were *partially buried–critical*; and the number *completely buried* using the definitions listed below.

133

The following definitions were composed for the purpose of reporting incidents and accidents with the intent of delineating between different rescue scenarios.

A person is *caught* if they are touched and adversely affected by the avalanche. People performing slope cuts are generally not considered *caught* in the resulting avalanche unless they are carried down the slope.

A person is *partially buried–not critical* if their head is above the snow surface when the avalanche stops.

A person is *partially buried–critical* if their head is below the snow surface when the avalanche stops but equipment, clothing and/or portions of their body are visible.

A person is *completely buried* if they are completely beneath the snow surface when the avalanche stops. Clothing and attached equipment are not visible on the surface.

For people that were *completely buried* or *partially buried–critical,* estimate the length of time they were buried, the burial depth measured from the snow surface to their face, position of person (face up, face down, or sitting), the distance between multiple persons and distance from vehicle if applicable. Include the method of rescue used to find the victim (i.e. transceiver, exposed equipment, exposed body part, spot probe, probe line, voice, etc.).

H.4.5 Diagram
Provide a sketch, photograph, or digital image showing the outline of the avalanche, the deposit, and the locations of people, snowmobiles, and other equipment when the avalanche started and when it stopped. Include significant terrain features and avalanche path characteristics such as starting zones or terrain traps.

H.4.6 Avalanche Description
Fill in the appropriate fields as accurately as possible.

H.4.7 Comments
Briefly describe: events leading to the avalanche involvement; how the rescue was conducted; the injuries sustained; level of avalanche training of group members; and other information that may be significant. A description of the events and decision-making process leading up to the accident should be recorded.

H.5 Completing the Detailed Report
On the form enter the information in the spaces provided or tick off the multiple-choice statements.

Write "N/Av" if the information is not available or "N/App" if not applicable. Online versions of these forms can be found at www.avalanche.org, www.fsavalanche.com, and www.colorado.gov/avalanche.

Figure H.1 Terrain trap (photography by Bruce Tremper)

American Avalanche Association
Forest Service National Avalanche Center
Avalanche Incident Report: Short Form

Occurrence Date:(YYYYMMDD)_____ Time:(HHMM) _____

Reporting Party Name and Address: _____

Avalanche Characteristics:
- Type:_____ Aspect:_____
- Trigger _____ Slope Angle:_____
- Size: R__/D__ Elevation:_____ m / ft
- Sliding Surface (check one):
  ☐ In new ☐ New/old ☐ In old ☐ Ground

Location:
- State:_____ County:_____ Forest:_____
- Peak, Mtn Pass, or Drainage:_____
- Site Name:_____
- Lat/Lon or UTM:_____
- Datum:_____

Group	Number of People	Time Recovered	Duration of Burial	Depth to Face ☐m ☐ft
Caught				
Partially Buried—Not-critical				
Partially Buried—Critical				
Completely Buried				

Number of people injured:_____ Number of people killed:_____

Dimensions: ☐m ☐ft	Average	Maximum
Height of Crown Face		
Width of Fracture		
Vertical fall		

Snow	Hardness	Grain Type	Grain Size
Slab			
Weak Layer			
Bed Surface			

Thickness of weak layer:_____ mm / cm / in

Burial involved a terrain trap? ☐ no ☐ yes→type:_____ Number of people that crossed start zone before the avalanche:_____
Location of group in relation to start zone during avalanche: ☐high ☐middle ☐low ☐below ☐ all ☐ unknown Avalanche occurred during: ☐ ascent ☐ descent

Subject	Name	Age	Gender	Address	Phone	Activity
1						
2						
3						
4						
5						

Equipment Carried
1 2 3 4 5
☐☐☐☐☐ transceiver
☐☐☐☐☐ shovel
☐☐☐☐☐ probe pole
☐☐☐☐☐ _____
☐☐☐☐☐ _____

Experience at Activity
1 2 3 4 5
☐☐☐☐☐ unknown
☐☐☐☐☐ novice
☐☐☐☐☐ intermediate
☐☐☐☐☐ advanced
☐☐☐☐☐ expert

Avalanche Training
1 2 3 4 5
☐☐☐☐☐ unknown
☐☐☐☐☐ none
☐☐☐☐☐ some
☐☐☐☐☐ advanced
☐☐☐☐☐ expert

Signs of Instability Noted by Group
☐ unknown
☐ none
☐ recent avalanches
☐ shooting cracks
☐ collapse or whumphing
☐ low test scores

Injuries Sustained
1 2 3 4 5
☐☐☐☐☐ none
☐☐☐☐☐ first aid
☐☐☐☐☐ doctor's care
☐☐☐☐☐ hospital stay
☐☐☐☐☐ fatal

Extent of Injuries or Cause of Death
1 2 3 4 5
☐☐☐☐☐ asphyxiation
☐☐☐☐☐ head trauma
☐☐☐☐☐ spinal injury
☐☐☐☐☐ chest trauma
☐☐☐☐☐ skeletal fractures
☐☐☐☐☐ _____

Damage Number of Vehicles Caught:_____ Number of Structures Damaged:_____ Estimated $ Loss:_____

Accident Summary Include: events leading to accident, group's familiarity with location, objectives, route, hazard evaluation, etc.

Rescue Summary Include: description of initial search, report of accident, organized rescue etc.

Rescue Method:
1 2 3 4 5
☐☐☐☐☐ self rescue
☐☐☐☐☐ transceiver
☐☐☐☐☐ spot probe
☐☐☐☐☐ probe line
☐☐☐☐☐ rescue dog
☐☐☐☐☐ voice
☐☐☐☐☐ object
☐☐☐☐☐ digging
☐☐☐☐☐ other_____

Attach additional pages as needed. Include: weather history, snow profiles, reports from other agencies, diagram of site, and any other supporting information.

Please send to: CAIC; 325 Broadway WS1; Boulder, CO 80305; caic@qwestoffic.net
Voice:(303) 499-9650 Fax (303) 499-9618 www.colorado.gov/avalanche

Snow, Weather, and Avalanches

American Avalanche Association
Forest Service National Avalanche Center
Avalanche Accident Report: Long Form

Please send to:
Colorado Avalanche Information Center
325 Broadway WS1
Boulder, CO 80305
voice: (303) 499-9650, fax: (303) 499-9618 fax, email: caic@qwestoffice.net, web: www.colorado.gov/avalanche

Occurrence Date:_____ **Time:**_____

Report Author(s):
Name:_____ Affiliation_____
Address:_____
_____
Phone:_____ Fax:_____ Email:_____

Location:
State:_____ County:_____ Region:_____ Forest:_____
Geographic Area (mountain range, mountain pass, drainage, or feature):_____
_____
Site Name:_____
Lat/Lon or UTM:_____ Elevation: ☐ above treeline ☐ near treeline ☐ below treeline
Datum:_____

Summary	Caught	Partially Buried Not-critical	Partially Buried Critical	Completely Buried	Injured	Killed	Vehicles Damaged	Structures Damaged
Number								

Weather	Fill in the weather chart of the five days prior to the accident. Use 24 hr averages or trends for wind speed and direction.

Weather station(s): Location_____ Lat/Lon or UTM:_____ Elevation:_____ m / ft

Date					Day of Accident
Tmax					
Tmin					
HN24					
HN24W					
Wind Speed					
Wind Dir					

Avalanche Conditions	Attach most recent avalanche advisory

Closest Avalanche Center:	Avalanche Danger Rating	Recent Avalanche Activity
_____	☐ Low	
☐ accident outside of forecast area	☐ Moderate ☐ Considerable ☐ High ☐ Extreme	
Avalanche warning in effect? ☐ yes ☐ no		

Snowpack	Describe the state of the snowpack. Include season history, snow profiles, and prominent features as necessary.

Section I: Group Information

Fill in the following tables. Some of the fields can be checked yes or left blank. Attach additional pages and reports from other agencies as necessary.

Subject	Name	Age	Gender	Address	Phone
1					
2					
3					
4					
5					

Skill Level	Activity	Years at Activity	Rank skill level as novice, intermediate, advanced, or expert.		Years Traveling in Avalanche Terrain	Avalanche Education Level
			Activity Skill Level	Accessed Local Avalanche Advisory		
1						
2						
3						
4						
5						

Rescue Equipment Carried	Transceiver Make and Model	Shovel	Probe Pole	Releasable Bindings	Other	Snowmobile: Rescue Equipment Carried on Person
1						
2						
3						
4						
5						

Injuries or Cause of Death	Unknown	None	First-Aid Necessary	Doctor's Care Needed	Hospital Stay Required	Asphyxia	Head Injury	Chest Injuries	Spinal Injury	Hypothermia	Skeletal Fracture	Other	Fatal
1													
2													
3													
4													
5													

Comments

Section II: Avalanche Path and Event Information

Fill in the following tables. Some of the fields can be checked yes or left blank. Attach additional pages, fracture line profiles, and reports as necessary.

Avalanche Characteristics

Type:_____ Trigger:_____ Size: □R1 □R2 □R3 □R4 □R5 / □D1 □D2 □D3 □D4 □D5

Sliding Surface (check one): □Within new snow □New/old interface □Old snow layer □Ground   □Avalanche stepped down into old snow layers.

Distance from trigger to crown face:_____ □m □ ft

Comments:

Dimensions

Dimensions □m □ft	Average	Maximum	Measured
Height of Crown Face			
Width			
Vertical fall			

Snow

Snow	Hardness	Grain Type	Grain Size	Thickness
Slab				
Weak Layer				
Bed Surface				

Start Zone

Elevation: _____ m / ft

Average Slope Angle (°) :_____

Maximum Slope Angle (°) :_____

Aspect:_____

Vegetation:_____

Ground Cover
- □ Smooth
- □ Rocky
- □ Glacier
- □ Dense Forest
- □ Open Forest
- □ Brush
- □ Grass
- □ Unknown

Location of Crown Face
- □ Ridge
- □ Cornice
- □ Mid-slope
- □ Convex Roll
- □ Concave Slope
- □ Rocks
- □ Unknown

Snow Moisture
- □ Dry
- □ Moist
- □ Wet

Track

- □ Open Slope   Average Slope Angle (°):_____
- □ Confined   Aspect:_____
- □ Gully

Snow Moisture   □Dry   □Moist   □Wet

Runout

Elevation: _____ m / ft

Average Incline (°) :_____

Aspect:_____

Vegetation:_____

Ground Cover
- □ Smooth
- □ Rocky
- □ Glacier
- □ Dense Forest
- □ Open Forest
- □ Brush
- □ Grass
- □ Unknown

Snow Moisture
- □ Dry
- □ Moist
- □ Wet

Debris Type
(check all that apply)
- □ Fine
- □ Blocks
- □ Hard
- □ Soft
- □ Rocks
- □ Trees
- □ _____
- □ _____

a_i (°) :_____

a_e(°) :_____

Debris Density:_____ kg/m^3

Terrain Trap: □no □yes

Terrain Trap Type:_____

Comments

Section III: Accident Description

Fill in the following sections with available information. Attach additional pages, statements, witness accounts, and other reports as necessary.

Events Leading Up to the Avalanche	Include objectives of party, departure point, route taken, familiarity with area, and encounters with other groups, location of party at time of avalanche, etc.

Location of group in relation to start zone at the time of avalanche release: ☐high ☐middle ☐low ☐below ☐all ☐unknown
Slope angle at approximate trigger site:_____°

Avalanche Danger Evaluation

Number of snowpit observations :_____   Stability Tests Performed: Test Results

Signs of Instability Observed:
☐ none   ☐ unknown   ☐ yes
☐ some cracking   ☐ shooting cracks   ☐ no
☐ whumphing   ☐ hollow sounds   ☐ unknown
☐ recent avalanche activity

Location of observations:_____

Comments

Witnesses	Name	Address	Phone
1			
2			

Accident Diagram	On a separate page or on a photograph, draw a diagram of the accident scene. Include avalanche boundaries, prominent rock and/or trees, the location of all party members before the avalanche, and the location of people, machines and equipment after the avalanche.

Section IV: Rescue

Fill in the following sections with available information. Attach additional pages, statements, witness accounts, and other reports as necessary.

Rescue Chronology

First Report	Response					
Reporting Party:	Agency	Time Dispatched	Time on Scene	Method of Travel	Number of Rescuers	Equipment
_____						
Report Method:						
_____						
Time Reported:_____						

Recovery

For Body Position use: Prone/Face Down, Supine/On Back, On Side, Sitting, Standing
For Head Position use: Up Hill, Down Hill, Sideways

Subject	Caught	Partially Buried - Non-critical	Partially Buried - Critical	Completely Buried	Depth to Face ☐m ☐ft	Time Recovered	Length of Burial	Body Position	Head Position
1									
2									
3									
4									
5									

Recovery Method

For a transceiver recovery, include make and model of transceiver used by searcher. If an object on the surface was used as a clue, list the object.

Subject	Self Rescue	Companion	Organized	Voice	Object	Transceiver	Spot Probe	Probe Line	Rescue Dog	Digging
1										
2										
3										
4										
5										

Rescue Description

List pertinent events that occurred during the rescue. Include additional pages of dispatch notes, statements, and agency reports as needed.

Section V: Damage

Fill in the following sections with available information. Attach additional pages, statements, witness accounts, and other reports as necessary.

Vehicles in Avalanche
Fill in the table below. Describe and/or estimate the cost of the damage to each vehicle caught in the avalanche.

Type	Partially Buried	Completely Buried	Damage	Replacement Cost

Structures Damaged
Fill in the table below. Describe and/or estimate the cost of the damage to each structure affected by the avalanche.

Type	Construction Type	Damage	Destroyed	Replacement Cost

Total Loss Estimate the cost of the damage caused by the avalanche. $_____

Rescue Cost Estimate the cost of rescue. $_____

Economic Effects List economic effects not included in the above tables (road closed, ski area closed, mine closed, change in policy, etc.)

Additional Comments and Recommendations

Appendix I
Symbols and Abbreviations

Symbol	Term	Units
BB	Boardblock test	categorical
CT	Compression test	categorical
D#	Avalanche size – destructive force	categorical
DT	Deep Tap Test	categorical
E	Grain size	mm
ECT	Extended column test	categorical
F	Grain form	categorical
f	Fall height of the hammer, ram penetrometer	cm
H	Vertical coordinate (line of plumb)	cm, m
H	Mass of hammer, ram penetrometer	kg
H2D/H2DW	Twice per day snow accumulation/water equivalent	cm/mm
HIN/HINW	Interval snow height/water equivalent	cm/mm
HN24/HN24W	Height of 24-hour snow accumulation/water equivalent	cm/mm
HN/HNW	Height of new snow layer/water equivalent	cm/mm
HS/HSW	Height of snowpack/total water equivalent	cm/mm
HST/HSTW	Storm snow height/water equivalent	cm/mm
HW	Water equivalent of a layer	mm
L	Layer thickness (measured vertically)	mm,cm,m
n	Number of blows of the hammer, ram penetrometer	dimensionless
N/O	Not observed	catagorical
P	Penetrability	cm
p	Increment of penetration for n blows, ram penetrometer	cm
PF	Depth of foot penetration	cm
PR	Depth of penetration by standard ramsonde	cm
PS	Depth of ski penetration	cm
PST	Propagation saw test	categorical
Q	Shear quality	categorical
R	Hand hardness index	categorical

Appendix I: Symbols and Abbreviations

Symbol	Term	Units
R#	Avalanche size – relative to path	categorical
RB	Rutschblock test	categorical
RH	Relative humidity	%
RN	Ram number	kg
RR	Ram resistance	N
SB	Stuffblock test	categorical
SR	Stability ratio	dimensionless
ST	Shovel shear test	categorical
T	Temperature of snow	°C
T	Mass of tubes, ram penetrometer	kg
Ta	Air temperature	°C
Tg	Ground temperature	°C
Ts	Temperature of snow surface	°C
T20	Temperature of snow 20 cm below the surface	°C
α	Alpha angle	degree
α_i	Alpha angle of an individual avalanche	degree
α_e	Alpha angle of an extreme event. Smallest angle observed in a specific avalanche path	degree
Δ (Delta)	Change in penetration	cm
ε (epsilon)	Strain	dimensionless (m/m)
θ (theta)	Liquid water content	% (by volume)
ρ (rho)	Density	kg/m^3
σ (sigma)	Normal stress	Pa
Σ (Sigma)	Normal strength	Pa
τ (tau)	Shear stress	Pa
T (Tau)	Shear strength	Pa
T_∞	Frame independent shear strength	Pa
T_{100}	Shear strength measured with 100 cm^2 shear frame	Pa
T_{250}	Shear strength measured with 250 cm^2 shear frame	Pa
ψ (psi)	Slope angle	degree

Snow, Weather, and Avalanches

Snow Profile

Reference:_____

Date: _____ Time: _____ Observers: _____

Location:_____

Elev: _____ Aspect: _____ Slope Angle: _____ Precip: _____ Sky: _____ Wind Dir: _____ Speed: _____G____

Blowing Snow: Ext ____ Dir ____ Loc _____ PS: _____ cm in PF: _____ cm in   Profile Type: [   ]

Snow Layer Temperature (°C)	Depth H	Moist θ	Form F	Size E	Density ρ	Test Results and Comments
-18° -16° -14° -12° -10° -8° -6° -4° -2°C	(cm)			(mm)	(kg/m³)	
	200					
	190					
	180					
	170					
	160					
	150					
	140					
	130					
	120					
	110					
	100					
	90					
	80					
	70					
	60					
	50					
	40					
	30					
	20					
	10					
	0					

I   K   P   1F   4F F

Snow, Weather, and Avalanches

Snow Profile

Reference:_____

Date: _____ Time: _____ Observers: _____

Location:_____

Elev: _____ Aspect: _____ Slope Angle: _____ Precip: _____ Sky: _____ Wind Dir: _____ Speed: _____ G ____

Blowing Snow: Ext ____ Dir ____ Loc _____ PS: _____ cm in PF: _____ cm in Profile Type: [_____]

Snow Layer Temperature (°C)	Depth H (cm)	Moist θ	Form F	Size E (mm)	Density ρ (kg/m³)	Test Results and Comments

I   K   P   1F   4F F

Snow, Weather, and Avalanches

Appendix I: Symbols and Abbreviations

Temperature Conversion Chart

°C	°F		°C	°F
-40	-40		0	32
-39	-38.2		1	33.8
-38	-36.4		2	35.6
-37	-34.6		3	37.4
-36	-32.8		4	39.2
-35	-31		5	41
-34	-29.2		6	42.8
-33	-27.4		7	44.6
-32	-25.6		8	46.4
-31	-23.8		9	48.2
-30	-22		10	50
-29	-20.2		11	51.8
-28	-18.4		12	53.6
-27	-16.6		13	55.4
-26	-14.8		14	57.2
-25	-13		15	59
-24	-11.2		16	60.8
-23	-9.4		17	62.6
-22	-7.6		18	64.4
-21	-5.8		19	66.2
-20	-4		20	68
-19	-2.2		21	69.8
-18	-0.4		22	71.6
-17	1.4		23	73.4
-16	3.2		24	75.2
-15	5		25	77
-14	6.8		26	78.8
-13	8.6		27	80.6
-12	10.4		28	82.4
-11	12.2		29	84.2
-10	14		30	86
-9	15.8		31	87.8
-8	17.6		32	89.6
-7	19.4		33	91.4
-6	21.2		34	93.2
-5	23		35	95
-4	24.8		36	96.8
-3	26.6		37	98.6
-2	28.4		38	100.4
-1	30.2		39	102.2
0	32		40	104

Snow, Weather, and Avalanches

Wind Speed Conversion Chart

mi/hr	m/s	kt	km/hr
1	0.4	0.9	1.6
2	0.9	1.7	3.2
3	1.3	2.6	4.8
4	1.8	3.5	6.4
5	2.2	4.3	8.0
10	4.5	8.7	16.1
15	6.7	13.0	24.1
20	8.9	17.4	32.2
25	11.2	21.7	40.2
30	13.4	26.1	48.3
35	15.6	30.4	56.3
40	17.9	34.8	64.4
45	20.1	39.1	72.4
50	22.4	43.4	80.5
55	24.6	47.8	88.5
60	26.8	52.1	96.6
65	29.1	56.5	104.6
70	31.3	60.8	112.7
75	33.5	65.2	120.7
80	35.8	69.5	128.7
85	38.0	73.9	136.8
90	40.2	78.2	144.8
95	42.5	82.6	152.9
100	44.7	86.9	160.9
105	46.9	91.2	169.0
110	49.2	95.6	177.0
115	51.4	99.9	185.1
120	53.6	104.3	193.1
125	55.9	108.6	201.2
130	58.1	113.0	209.2
135	60.4	117.3	217.3
140	62.6	121.7	225.3
145	64.8	126.0	233.4
150	67.1	130.3	241.4

Appendix I: Symbols and Abbreviations

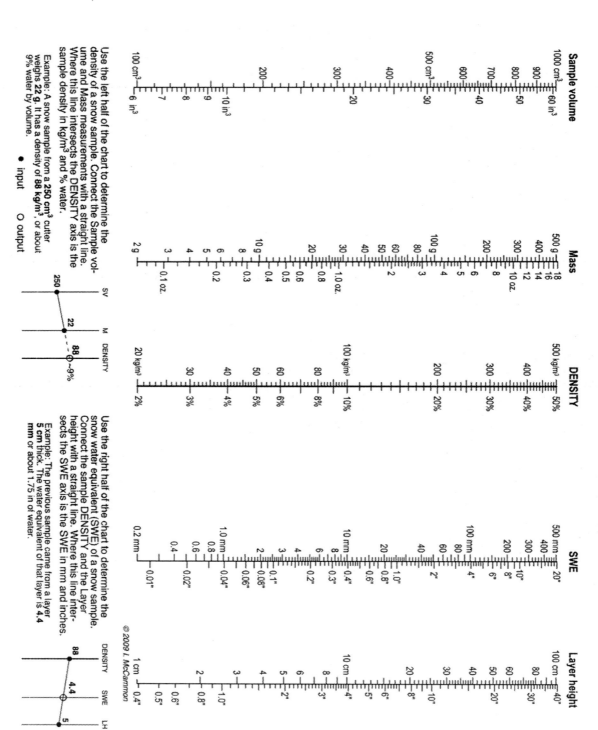

Nomogram for determining snow density and snow water equivalent (SWE)

© 2009 I. McCammon

150